John

A Tool for Making Disciples Who Make Disciples

by

r. j. arthur
under shepherd, teacher, author, lecturer, student

John: A Tool for Making Disciples Who Make Disciples

ISBN: 978-1492170136

Printed in the United States of America

John

_____
name

Table of Content

Subject:

- The fourth book in the New Testament: The book of John

Books and Materials:

- The workbook of *John*

- The ESV® Study Bible (i.e. English Standard Version)

The John Study Objectives:

- To encourage self-discipline with *daily reading* and *daily studying* of the scriptures.

- To learn how to use the tools found in the ESV Study Bible (i.e. cross-references; footnotes; commentary notes; maps; charts; concordance; etc.).

- To develop the proper method of interpretation in order to "handle accurately the word of truth."

- To provide deeper insight into the truths found in the book of *John* in order to develop one's personal relationship with God through Jesus the Christ.

- And possibly most important, all of the above objectives are designed to be easily reproduced from one disciple to another. Obedience to Jesus Christ is the greatest objective. Jesus has commanded us to make disciples. This study is designed as a discipleship tool so believers can pursue obedience. Every disciple that goes through this study will be able to take other future disciples through this study, and then teach them to obey by doing the same, and so on, and so on.

How To Use This Study:

- The book of John has been divided into sixteen sessions. Each session has a passage followed by a series of questions pertaining to that particular passage.

- The questions are designed to help the disciple of Christ develop a proper method of interpreting the scriptures by learning how to literally and consistently use the following: context; grammatical structure; and historical setting. The questions are also designed to develop the skills in using the tools of the ESV Study Bible (i.e. cross-references; footnotes; commentary notes; maps; charts; concordance; etc.).

- The order of the questions directly corresponds to the order of the text. There are basically three types of questions:

    1). Questions directly quoted from the scriptures. The portion of the question that is directly quoted from the scriptures will be in quotation marks.

    2). Questions where the answers should come directly from the text. The answer to these questions should be worded, if not directly quoted, from the scriptures.

    3). "What do you think" questions. These questions may not have a direct answer from the text but the student should use the text to support the reason for their answer.

- The student of the Bible should try to read the provided scripture within the workbook (i.e. the passage with no chapters or verses) in one sitting several times throughout the week. The student should also daily use the ESV Study Bible to utilize various tools, as well as reference chapters and verses, to answers the questions of each session.

Truth

What Is Truth?

What is Truth? Truth is defined in the Webster's Dictionary as "that which is true; a fact; a reality; that which conforms to fact or reality; the real or true state of things." There are various categories or kinds of truth. For example, there is mathematical truth (e.g. 2 + 2 = 4); scientific truth (e.g. gravity); personal perspective truth (e.g. the type of foods one may like); and spiritual truth (e.g. God created everything). Each of these various categories of truth has their place of importance. Each of these categories also has their own path or methods for pursuing the truth and confirming their fact or reality.

The Importance of Spiritual Truth

Spiritual realities affects every single person. In fact, this short life here on earth will actually determine each soul's eternal destiny. Everyone will exist forever; the question is where and in what kind of eternal state? This is a serious sobering proposition. Everyone, whether they acknowledge it or not, will stand before God and give an account for the spiritual truth they know and how they lived according to that truth (Ecclesiastes 12:14 with Philippians 2:11). But the importance of spiritual truth goes far beyond one's personal interest or even where they will spend eternity.

Spiritual truth is important because God is the most important. He is worthy of knowing, honoring, and serving. The only way to get to know the one true holy God is through pure absolute spiritual truth. We are all accountable to God, if for no other reason, because He is our Creator. God created mankind to know and serve Him in order to glorify Him. The core purpose of your life is to know and obey God for His glory. And again, the only way to get to know God is through spiritual truth. The more spiritual truth one knows, the greater opportunity one has to fulfill their life's purpose (i.e. know and obey God for His glory).

1

How to Know God

God has revealed Himself at many times in various ways, but in these last days He has made Himself known through a Person. In the past He has spoken spiritual truth through prophets, dreams, prophetesses, visions, tongues, miracles, the incarnate Christ, Apostles, audibly, scripture, through a donkey, etc. But in these last days, God reveals Himself to mankind through the Person of Jesus the Christ. "Long ago, at many times and in many ways, God spoke to our fathers by the prophets, but in these last days he has spoken to us by his Son…" (Hebrews 1:1-2a). Jesus is the exact imprint of God and is the only way that someone can know God. So the only way to know God is by knowing Jesus. And as previously stated, the more spiritual truth one knows, the greater opportunity one has to fulfill the purpose of their life (i.e. obey God for His glory). So if Jesus is the Truth and is the only way to know God, how can someone come to know Jesus?

There are two clear and distinct ideas concerning what it means to "know" Jesus. The first is to have intellectual knowledge about Jesus. This is to know intellectual aspects or facts concerning the Person of Jesus the Christ. The other is to have an intimate personal spiritual relationship with Jesus through true biblical faith. This is the relationship that every Christian has with God through Jesus the Christ. For either of the above meanings, the Bible is the only source for knowing Jesus. Even though it is the same source needed to know Jesus, each idea has its own method for knowing Him.

The only way to have a personal relationship with Jesus the Christ through true biblical faith, is if God himself teaches and reveals Jesus to the individual. Today, God's word is only spoken by the Holy Spirit. And the Holy Spirit only speaks through the truth of the Bible. Just like the incarnate Jesus only spoke the words of God the Father in order to reveal the Father, the Holy Spirit will only speak Jesus' words in order to reveal Jesus. (John 5:17-47; 6:44-65; 7:17-18; 8:12-59; 10:14-39; 12:49-50; 13:1-3; 14:6; 14:10; 14:26; 16:13-15). And as previously stated, the only way the Holy Spirit speaks is through the

truth of the Bible. This is not to say that someone cannot understand the truth of the Bible apart from the Holy Spirit. This latter point is referencing the first Idea about "intellectually knowing" truth and will be discussed later at length. But it is only possible to have an intimate personal spiritual relationship with Jesus through faith as the Holy Spirit speaks/reveals Jesus through the truth of the scriptures. In fact, it is only through the truth that is intellectually understood by an individual in which the Holy Spirit will spiritually speak into the individual's life through faith. This is why it is so imperative for people to know the truth (i.e. intellectually) in order for them to know The Truth (i.e. spiritual relationship with God through faith in Jesus). Presenting the following definition of terms may help simplify this often complicated subject:

Scripture: the actual sacred writings of the Bible. Anyone, from the atheist to most devout Christian, can equally intellectually understand the truth of the Scriptures. This is not to say that the truth of the scriptures will have the same effect on people; but simply, what the scriptures are proclaiming can be correctly understood.

God's Word: God's word is what God says when He speaks. As previously stated, God has spoken at many times and in various ways in the past. God the Father has spoken, God the Son has spoken, and today God the Holy Spirit is speaking. Today, God the Holy Spirit is only speaking through the truth of the scripture and only the Christian can hear and understand God's word. God's word is active, alive, sharper than a two-edged sword, never returns void, perfect as God because it is spoken from a perfect God, etc.

The Bible: The Bible can be referencing to either the Scriptures or to God's Word (this is where it can get a little confusing). Though the Scriptures and God's word are one and the same when referring to the material substance, they are very different when it comes to how they function; or in other words, cause and effect. This is why the Bible is often called God's word and is also used to reference the Scriptures. For instance, to open the Bible to John 3:16 would be using the term "the Bible" to reference the Scriptures.

How to Know the Truth of the Scriptures

Have you ever wondered why there are so many different kinds of churches or ideas about what the Bible says? It is because people have many different ways in which they approach the scriptures as they seek to know the truth. There is only one absolute Truth; therefore, there is only one correct way to approach the Bible to know that truth. Truth is not relative; therefore, the approach to know the truth is not relative either. The truth of the scriptures is knowable. With the correct approach, anyone can intellectually understand the intended truth of the Bible.

The student of the Bible must approach the scriptures with a consistent biblical method in order to consistently have a correct interpretation. In theology, a method of interpretation is referred to as a hermeneutic (hûr mə nū tǐk). "Hermeneutics is the study of the principles of interpretation. Exegesis consists of the actual interpretation of the Bible, the bringing out of its meaning, while hermeneutics establishes the principles by which exegesis is practiced. In actuality every interpreter of the Bible has a system of hermeneutics whether consciously so or not."[1] If two individuals had a similar hermeneutic, they would also have a similar interpretation of the Bible (i.e. exegesis). It is the hermeneutic that determines or dictates the interpretation. So the reason there are so many different ideas of what the Bible says, is due to a wide variety of different hermeneutics (i.e. methods of interpretation).

A person's method of interpretation is based on their definition of the Bible. In other words, how one defines the Bible will establish the guiding principles on how they approach and interpret the Bible. The following definition is what the Bible teaches about itself and will provide the method of interpretation for this study:

THE BIBLE: The sixty-six canonized books of the Old and New Testaments, as originally given, are the verbally inspired (i.e. God-

---

[1] Charles C. Ryrie, Basic Theology, p.110

breathed), plenary, infallible, inerrant, complete and sufficient perspicuous sole Word of God in this present Church age. The Bible, the whole Bible, and nothing but the Bible is a Christian's sole authority in all matters of faith, doctrine, and practice (2 Timothy 3:16-17; 2 Peter 1:20-21). "When Scripture speaks God speaks, when Scripture is not speaking God is not speaking."

There are at least two interrelated factors that will prevent a student of the Bible from correctly interpreting the perfect Bible. The first is the depravity of humanity due to a sin nature. Sin entered the world through Adam and has been inherited or passed on from generation to generation. This depravity will create prejudice and bias. The second factor preventing a student of the Bible from correctly interpreting the scriptures are the influences of the Adversary within our fallen or sinful environment. From the beginning until his end, Satan has and will continue to try to distort and pervert the truth. He will attempt to create misunderstanding and/or doubt of truth (Genesis 3:1b; Luke 4:10-11; John 8:44; Revelation 20:7-10). Though the Bible is knowable and true, humanity's sin nature along with the influences of the adversary often prevents the interpreter from correctly understanding the intended truth of the Bible. Even the most sincere and earnest Christian needs protection from misinterpreting the scriptures. These protections will be referred to as "hermeneutic safeguards."

The Holy Spirit is the perfect Teacher and Reminder of God's perfect Word. But as long as the Christian has a sin nature, and/or the influences of the adversary, there is a need for protection against misinterpretation. "Hermeneutic safeguards" will provide assurance that what is understood of scripture is the intended truth. And with this truth, the Christian can have complete confidence that the Holy Teacher of God will spiritually speak God's word and accomplish God's purpose in their lives.

There are several practical "hermeneutic safeguards" that originate from the previous definition of the Bible. The following

hermeneutic safeguards are developed and taught through this John study:

- **Context** – A student of Scripture must consider the context of a Bible passage within each passage, book, and whole of the Bible in order to properly understand the Bible.

- **Grammatical Structure** – The God of the Bible has chosen to communicate through language. The original language of the Old Testament was mostly Hebrew. The New Testament was Greek. Understanding the original languages will prove to be a valuable asset in properly understanding the Bible.

- **Historical Setting** – God used different men throughout two thousand years to write the Bible. Understanding the history of man's settings, culture, languages, circumstances and situations will help the student to properly understand the Bible.

- **Literal and Consistent principle of interpretation** – A consistent approach to Scripture will help protect the student from their prejudice or bias. To literally interpret God's Word is to literally understand the Scripture with the intent which God meant for Scripture to be interpreted. This is a difficult concept. For example, the Bible refers to different kinds of people as sheep and as goats (sheep being Christians and goats being non-Christians). Should the Bible student understand human beings to literally be four legged animals with wool? To understand Scripture in this manner would not be interpreting the Bible with the literal intent. God *consistently* says what He means and *literally* means what He says!

This study of John is part of a discipleship series that will develop the skills to use various tools in order to apply a proper biblical hermeneutic; thus, the student of the Bible will be able to confidently know the truth of the scriptures. The above hermeneutic safeguards will become understood and developed throughout this John study. As the student of the Bible continues to develop these

hermeneutic safeguards they will be able to confidently know the truth of the Bible. The goal is for every student of the Bible to develop the proper hermeneutic safeguards so they can solely depend upon the Holy Spirit to teach them the Bible; and then, be able to teach others to do the same.

Fill-In-The-Blank, Short Answer, Multiple Choice, and True or False

1.1 **"Spiritual truth is important because _____ is the most important"** (note: page 1, last paragraph. When the question or statement is in "quotes," then it is a direct quote found within the text)

1.2 **"The core purpose of your life is to _____ and _____ God for His glory"** (note: page 1, last paragraph. When the question or statement is in "quotes," then it is a direct quote found within the text)

2.1 **The only way to know God is by knowing the Person of _____ the Christ.**

2.2 **"The more spiritual _____ one knows, the greater opportunity one has to fulfill the _____ of their life (i.e. obey God for His glory)."** (note: page 1, last paragraph)

3.1 **The only way to have a personal relationship with Jesus through faith is for God the _____ _____ to reveal Jesus to the individual.** (note: page 2, last paragraph)

3.2 **The way that God the Holy Spirit speaks today is through** (circle all that apply)**:**

A. the truth of Scripture	E. a person's heart
B. a still small voice	F. anyway He chooses
C. prayer	G. the Bible
D. Jesus Christ's words	H. a person's understanding of the truth of the Bible

4.1 Scripture: "the actual sacred _____ of the Bible."

4.2 God's Word: "what God _____ when He _____."

4.3 The Bible: can refer to _____ or _____ _____.

5.0 In theology, a method of interpretation is called a

_____.

6.0 True or False: A person's method of interpretation is based on their definition of the Bible. (note: page 4, last paragraph)

7.0 What are two things that could prevent a Christian from correctly understanding the Scriptures?

    1).

    2).

8.0 List the proper hermeneutic safeguards that a person should follow in order to correctly interpret the Bible?

9.0 "This study of John is part of a discipleship series that will develop the _____ to use various _____ in order to apply a proper biblical_____ ; thus, the student of the Bible will be able to know the truth of the scriptures." And then the disciple of Christ can pass them on to others. (last paragraph)

8

Read the Introduction to the Book of John in the ESV Study Bible to help answer the following fill-in-the-blank. Use the following words to try and fill in the blanks on the following two pages. (hint: you may want to use a pencil in case you need to erase and/or change your answers.)

70

Andrew

baptism

birth

Characteristics

Date

demons

James

John

John

last

lepers

parables

Peter

synoptic

temptation

twelve

unique

upper room

Introduction

I. The Author, Date, and Characteristics of the Book of John. (Note: this information is important for various reasons which be explored at a later date. This information was also used by the early church fathers in determining the Book of John as part of the canon of Scripture.)

   A. The Author of the forth Book in the New Testament. He must have been one of the _____ disciples.

      1. He was present in the _____ _____ (John 13:23-25; 21:20 with Mark 14:15 and Luke 22:12)

      2. He was probably one of the three (occasionally four) disciples who were closest to Jesus – Peter, James, John, and sometimes Andrew (John 13:23; 19:26; 20:2; 21:20).

         a. We know that the person reclining next to Jesus was not _____, because he asked "the disciple whom Jesus loved" a question (John 13:24).

         b. The person was probably not _____, since he is explicitly named several times (John 1:40, 44; 6:8; 12:22). It would be inconsistent to name a disciple in some places and to list him anonymously as "the disciple whom Jesus loved" in others (most all the other disciples are mentioned by name as well, but John is never referred to by name).

         c. The person could not have been _____. This disciple died at the hands of Herod Agrippa I (Acts 12:2) early in the development of the church, and the fourth Gospel was written years after his death.

         d. Therefore, the most likely candidate is James' brother _____. Indeed, early church tradition is also unanimous that John the apostle, son of Zebedee, wrote the fourth Gospel we call John.

B. The _____ of the writing of the Book of John

    1. As is so often the case with books of the Bible, it is difficult to give an exact date for the writing of John's gospel. Traditionally most scholars agree that it was the _____ of the four gospels to be written.

    2. It was probably composed sometime between A.D. 80 or 90, though it could have been written shortly after the destruction of Jerusalem in A.D. _____.

C. The _____ of the Book of John. John's gospel is quite different than the synoptic Gospels (i.e. Matthew, Mark, and Luke).

    1. This is not to say that the gospel of _____ contradicts the _____ Gospels. Rather, John makes explicit to what Matthew, Mark, and Luke only allude. He also leaves out a lot of material covered in the Synoptic Gospels, but he adds information about aspects of Jesus' ministry not discussed elsewhere.

    2. Some _____ characteristics of the book of John

        a. The book of John does not describe the specifics of Jesus' _____, _____, or _____.

        b. Also, the book of John does not record Jesus casting out _____, curing _____, or Jesus speaking in _____.

Introduction

ESV Study Bible Notes

The purpose of the notes in the ESV Study Bible is to provide significant explanatory help for Christians who want to understand the Bible in a deeper way. To that end, the notes provide the following types of helpful content:

1. Explanation of the Bible text, especially with regard to the meaning of specific words and phrases in their immediate context and in relation to the Bible as a whole.
2. Brief summary notes at the beginning of each new section, explaining the meaning and purpose of the section. These correspond to the outline for each book of the Bible, and are shaded within the notes to help identify the structure of each book.
3. A summary of how specific Bible texts fit into the overall history of salvation as this unfolds throughout the Old Testament.
4. Explanation of puzzling events, words, and phrases that are often misunderstood.
5. Background descriptions of historical and archaeological information, providing a contextual framework to help illuminate and understand the text.
6. Explanation of key Greek and Hebrew words (usually given in their lexical form), to provide insight into the meaning of key words in the original languages of the Bible.
7. Presentation of significant alternative interpretations of important Bible passages.
8. Explanation of key texts that are crucial for the understanding of Christian doctrine, theology, and ethics.
9. Interaction with and responses to challenges concerning the truthfulness, historicity, or believability of specific Bible passages.
10. Application to life today for selected key passages.

Textual Footnotes

The footnotes that accompany the ESV text are an integral part of the ESV translation, informing the reader of textual variations and difficulties and showing how these have been resolved by the ESV translation team. In addition to this, the footnotes indicate significant alternative readings and occasionally provide an explanation for technical terms or for a difficult reading in the text.

Cross-reference system and Concordance

The ESV Study Bible includes 80,000 cross-references and an extensive concordance, which together encourage easy location of important words, passages, and biblical themes. There are several kinds of cross-references, for example:

- References to specific words or phrases appear as:
  "ver.20" (within the same chapter)
  "ch. 5:26" (within the same book)
  "Heb. 4:2" (when referencing a different book)
- Brackets denote passages with similar themes. For example:
  "[Col. 1:17]"
- "See" denotes less direct references. For example:
  "See ver 7" or "See ch. 11:52" or "See Deut. 18:15"
- "Cited" denotes passages quoted in or from other parts of Scripture. For example:
  "Cited from Ps. 69:9"
- "(Heb.)" or "(Gk.)" indicates that the similarity of a cross-referenced passage is clearer in the original Hebrew or Greek than in English.

John 1:1-18

In the beginning was the Word, and the Word was with God, and the Word was God. He was in the beginning with God. All things were made through him, and without him was not any thing made that was made. In him was life, and the life was the light of men. The light shines in the darkness, and the darkness has not overcome it.

There was a man sent from God, whose name was John. He came as a witness, to bear witness about the light, that all might believe through him. He was not the light, but came to bear witness about the light.

The true light, which gives light to everyone, was coming into the world. He was in the world, and the world was made through him, yet the world did not know him. He came to his own, and his own people did not receive him. But to all who did receive him, who believed in his name, he gave the right to become children of God, who were born, not of blood nor of the will of the flesh nor of the will of man, but of God.

And the Word became flesh and dwelt among us, and we have seen his glory, glory as of the only Son from the Father, full of grace and truth. (John bore witness about him, and cried out, "This was he of whom I said, 'He who comes after me ranks before me, because he was before me.'") For from his fullness we have all received, grace upon grace. For the law was given through Moses; grace and truth came through Jesus Christ. No one has ever seen God; except the only One, who is God, who is at the Father's side, he has made him known.

Session 1

1.1   **What other book in the Bible begins, "In the beginning ..."** (hint: you may want to refer to the cross reference labeled as "a")**?**

1.2   **In this other book, what's the next word in the opening verse?**

1.3   **What are the next three words in John 1:1?**

1.4   **What do you think the word "beginning" means in each use?**

2.0   **In reading John 1:1-18, to whom does the "Word" refer** (support your answer with proofs from the scriptures; for instance: personal pronouns; was the Word a person, place or thing; is His name given; etc.)**?**

3.1   **How can the Word be "with God" and also be "God"?** (note: you may want to refer to the ESV Study Bible Notes on John 1:1. Read the article in the introduction section to better learn about the ESV Study Bible Notes)[2]

3.2   **What fundamental doctrine does this begin to establish?**

4.1   **What was made through the Word?**

4.2   **Without the Word, what was "made that was made?"**

5.0   **Who was coming "to bear witness about the [true] light?"**

---

[2] To better understand the features of the ESV Study Bible Notes read about this study tool in the Introduction and Preface sections located at the beginning of the study Bible under the sections titled, "The Purpose of the ESV Study Bible Notes."

additional notes

6.0 In John 1:10, what do you think the word "world" means in each of its three uses?

7.1 How does someone have "the right to become children of God" or be born of God?

7.2 What do you think this means (hint: you may want to refer to the ESV Study Notes)?

8.1 What was given through Moses?

8.2 What came through Jesus Christ?

8.3 How do you think these two differ from one another and how do you think they are similar?

9.1 In John 1:18, who is the only human being to see God? (note: you may want to refer to the textual footnotes, ESV Study Bible Notes, and the cross-references for "the only Son" in verses 14 and 18. Read the articles in the introduction section to better learn about the textual footnotes and cross-references system)[3]

9.2 What has He done?

9.3 What did God tell Moses in Exodus 33:20, when Moses asked to see God?

9.4 How do you reconcile these two passages (i.e. God said no one could see Him and live, yet Jesus Christ has fully seen Him)?

---

[3] To better understand the features of the "Cross-reference System," and "Textual Footnotes" read about these study tools in the Introduction and Preface sections located at the beginning of the study Bible under the sections titled, "Using the Cross-reference System" and "Textual Footnotes."

additional notes

Session 2

And this is the testimony of John, when the Jews sent priests and Levites from Jerusalem to ask him, "Who are you?" He confessed, and did not deny, but confessed, "I am not the Christ." And they asked him, "What then? Are you Elijah?" He said, "I am not." "Are you the Prophet?" And he answered, "No." So they said to him, "Who are you? We need to give an answer to those who sent us. What do you say about yourself?" He said, "I am the voice of one crying out in the wilderness, 'Make straight the way of the Lord,' as the prophet Isaiah said."

(Now they had been sent from the Pharisees.) They asked him, "Then why are you baptizing, if you are neither the Christ, nor Elijah, nor the Prophet?" John answered them, "I baptize with water, but among you stands one you do not know, even he who comes after me, the strap of whose sandal I am not worthy to untie." These things took place in Bethany across the Jordan, where John was baptizing.

The next day he saw Jesus coming toward him, and said, "Behold, the Lamb of God, who takes away the sin of the world! This is he of whom I said, 'After me comes a man who ranks before me, because he was before me.' I myself did not know him, but for this purpose I came baptizing with water, that he might be revealed to Israel." And John bore witness: "I saw the Spirit descend from heaven like a dove, and it remained on him. I myself did not know him, but he who sent me to baptize with water said to me, 'He on whom you see the Spirit descend and remain, this is he who baptizes with the Holy Spirit.' And I have seen and have borne witness that this is the Son of God."

The next day again John was standing with two of his disciples, and he looked at Jesus as he walked by and said, "Behold, the Lamb of God!" The two disciples heard him say this, and they followed Jesus. Jesus turned and saw them following and said to them, "What are you seeking?" And they said to him, "Rabbi" (which means Teacher), "where are you staying?" He said to them, "Come and you

will see." So they came and saw where he was staying, and they stayed with him that day, for it was about the tenth hour. One of the two who heard John speak and followed Jesus was Andrew, Simon Peter's brother. He first found his own brother Simon and said to him, "We have found the Messiah" (which means Christ). He brought him to Jesus. Jesus looked at him and said, "You are Simon the son of John. You shall be called Cephas" (which means Peter).

The next day Jesus decided to go to Galilee. He found Philip and said to him, "Follow me." Now Philip was from Bethsaida, the city of Andrew and Peter. Philip found Nathanael and said to him, "We have found him of whom Moses in the Law and also the prophets wrote, Jesus of Nazareth, the son of Joseph." Nathanael said to him, "Can anything good come out of Nazareth?" Philip said to him, "Come and see." Jesus saw Nathanael coming toward him and said of him, "Behold, an Israelite indeed, in whom there is no deceit!" Nathanael said to him, "How do you know me?" Jesus answered him, "Before Philip called you, when you were under the fig tree, I saw you." Nathanael answered him, "Rabbi, you are the Son of God! You are the King of Israel!" Jesus answered him, "Because I said to you, 'I saw you under the fig tree,' do you believe? You will see greater things than these." And he said to him, "Truly, truly, I say to you, you will see heaven opened, and the angels of God ascending and descending on the Son of Man."

Session 2

1.1 **When questioned about his identity, who did John the Baptist say he wasn't, who he was, and the significance of each?** (note: you may want to use the cross-reference system to understand where John got his answer and the context of that passage. You may also want to use the ESV Study Bible Notes and references to understand why they asked him if he were the expected individuals.)

1.2 **After John revealed his identity, why do you think the Jews questioned John on why he was baptizing?**

2.1 **What did John baptize with?**

2.2 **What did he say Jesus baptizes with?**

3.1 **What did John the Baptist call Jesus when "he saw Jesus coming toward him"?**

3.2 **What did John the Baptist mean in John 1:30** (note: you may want to refer to the first couple of questions in Session 1)**?**

4.0 **What did John the Baptist say his "purpose" was for baptizing with water?**

5.0 **How was the identity of the Son of God made known to John?**

additional notes

Session 2

6.0 **According to John 1:39, what time** (present day time) **was it after the disciples saw where Jesus was staying and spent the day with Him** (note: you may want to refer to the footnote)**?**

A. 10:00 pm	C. 4:00 pm
B. 10:00 am	D. Other _____

7.0 **Who do you think John's two disciples were in John 1:35?**

8.0 **What was the first thing Andrew did after he had followed Jesus?**

9.1 **What town were Philip, Andrew, and Peter from?**

9.2 **Assuming the "Bethany across the Jordan" was located near where the Jordan river emptied into the Dead Sea, approximately how far is the fishing town where Philip, Andrew, and Peter lived from where Jesus was baptized** (note: you may want to refer to the map located in the "INTRODUCTION TO JOHN")**?**

10.1 **How did Jesus describe Nathanael?**

10.2 **What three names did Nathanael call Jesus?**

10.3 **What do you think each of these names mean?**

additional notes

John 2:1-25

On the third day there was a wedding at Cana in Galilee, and the mother of Jesus was there. Jesus also was invited to the wedding with his disciples. When the wine ran out, the mother of Jesus said to him, "They have no wine." And Jesus said to her, "Woman, what does this have to do with me? My hour has not yet come." His mother said to the servants, "Do whatever he tells you."

Now there were six stone water jars there for the Jewish rites of purification, each holding twenty or thirty gallons. Jesus said to the servants, "Fill the jars with water." And they filled them up to the brim. And he said to them, "Now draw some out and take it to the master of the feast." So they took it. When the master of the feast tasted the water now become wine, and did not know where it came from (though the servants who had drawn the water knew), the master of the feast called the bridegroom and said to him, "Everyone serves the good wine first, and when people have drunk freely, then the poor wine. But you have kept the good wine until now." This, the first of his miraculous signs, Jesus did at Cana in Galilee, and manifested his glory. And his disciples believed in him.

After this he went down to Capernaum, with his mother and his brothers and his disciples, and they stayed there for a few days.

The Passover of the Jews was at hand, and Jesus went up to Jerusalem. In the temple he found those who were selling oxen and sheep and pigeons, and the money-changers sitting there. And making a whip of cords, he drove them all out of the temple, with the sheep and oxen. And he poured out the coins of the money-changers and overturned their tables. And he told those who sold the pigeons, "Take these things away; do not make my Father's house a house of trade." His disciples remembered that it was written, "Zeal for your house will consume me."

So the Jews said to him, "What sign do you show us for doing these things?" Jesus answered them, "Destroy this temple, and in three days I will raise it up." The Jews then said, "It has taken forty-six

years to build this temple, and will you raise it up in three days?" But he was speaking about the temple of his body. When therefore he was raised from the dead, his disciples remembered that he had said this, and they believed the Scripture and the word that Jesus had spoken.

Now when he was in Jerusalem at the Passover Feast, many believed in his name when they saw the signs that he was doing. But Jesus on his part did not entrust himself to them, because he knew all people and needed no one to bear witness about man, for he himself knew what was in man.

Session 3

1.1 **What was Jesus' response when His mother told Him "they have no wine?"**

1.2 **Why do you think he responded this way?** (Hint: you may want to use the cross-references and notes referencing Jesus' phrase, "My hour has not yet come." Note: whenever references to specific words or phrases appear within the same book, they have the letters "ch." followed by the chapter and verse. For example, ch. 7:30, 8:20, 13:1)

2.1 **What did wine symbolically represent in Jesus' last supper** (i.e. Matthew 26:26-29; Mark 14:22-25; Luke 22:18-20)?

2.2 **What was Jesus' first miraculous sign?**

2.3 **About how many gallons of water, and in what kind of containers, did Jesus turn into wine?**

2.4 **What was the quality of this wine?**

3.1 **What was "manifested" by Jesus performing the first of His signs?**

3.2 **How did Jesus' disciples respond to this incident** (note: you may want to refer to the ESV Study Notes on John 2:11)?

4.1 **Where did Jesus perform His first miraculous sign?**

4.2 **Where, and in what direction, did He travel next** (note: you may want to refer to the map located in the "INTRODUCTION TO JOHN")?

4.3 **Where, and in what direction, did He travel next when it was almost time for the Jewish Passover** (note: you may want to refer to the map located in the "INTRODUCTION TO JOHN")?

4.4 **How do you explain "went down" in John 2:12 and "went up" in John 2:13?**

additional notes

Session 3

5.1   **Why do you think people would sell animals during the Jewish Passover?**

5.2   **Why do you think there were people exchanging currencies?**

6.0   **How many times did Jesus clear the temple during His earthly ministry?** (Note: you may want to utilize the cross-references of John 2:14. When cross-references are in [brackets] it denotes passages with a similar theme. Notice the chronological time frame; that is, beginning or end of Christ's earthly ministry, of when Christ clears the temple in the other synoptic gospel accounts that are found in the cross-reference of the John 2:14-17 passage.)

7.1   **What miraculous sign did Jesus say He would show to prove His authority?**

7.2   **What temple did the Jews think Jesus was referencing?**

7.3   **What temple was He actually speaking of?**

7.4   **After Jesus was raised from the dead, what effect did these words have on the disciples?**

8.1   **How did many respond to Jesus "when they saw the signs that he was doing"?**

8.2   **How did Jesus respond to these people?**

8.3   **Why do you think Jesus responded this way?**

additional notes

Session 4

$$\boxed{\text{John 3:1 - 4:3}}$$

Now there was a man of the Pharisees named Nicodemus, a ruler of the Jews. This man came to Jesus by night and said to him, "Rabbi, we know that you are a teacher come from God, for no one can do these signs that you do unless God is with him." Jesus answered him, "Truly, truly, I say to you, unless one is born again he cannot see the kingdom of God." Nicodemus said to him, "How can a man be born when he is old? Can he enter a second time into his mother's womb and be born?" Jesus answered, "Truly, truly, I say to you, unless one is born of water and the Spirit, he cannot enter the kingdom of God. That which is born of the flesh is flesh, and that which is born of the Spirit is spirit. Do not marvel that I said to you, 'You must be born again.' The wind blows where it wishes, and you hear its sound, but you do not know where it comes from or where it goes. So it is with everyone who is born of the Spirit."

Nicodemus said to him, "How can these things be?" Jesus answered him, "Are you the teacher of Israel and yet you do not understand these things? Truly, truly, I say to you, we speak of what we know, and bear witness to what we have seen, but you do not receive our testimony. If I have told you earthly things and you do not believe, how can you believe if I tell you heavenly things? No one has ascended into heaven except he who descended from heaven, the Son of Man. And as Moses lifted up the serpent in the wilderness, so must the Son of Man be lifted up, that whoever believes in him may have eternal life.

"For God so loved the world, that he gave his only Son, that whoever believes in him should not perish but have eternal life. For God did not send his Son into the world to condemn the world, but in order that the world might be saved through him. Whoever believes in him is not condemned, but whoever does not believe is condemned already, because he has not believed in the name of the only Son of God. And this is the judgment: the light has come into the world, and people loved the darkness rather than the light because

30

John 3:1 - 4:3

their works were evil. For everyone who does wicked things hates the light and does not come to the light, lest his works should be exposed. But whoever does what is true comes to the light, so that it may be clearly seen that his works have been carried out in God."

After this Jesus and his disciples went into the Judean countryside, and he remained there with them and was baptizing. John also was baptizing at Aenon near Salim, because water was plentiful there, and people were coming and being baptized (for John had not yet been put in prison).

Now a discussion arose between some of John's disciples and a Jew over purification. And they came to John and said to him, "Rabbi, he who was with you across the Jordan, to whom you bore witness— look, he is baptizing, and all are going to him." John answered, "A person cannot receive even one thing unless it is given him from heaven. You yourselves bear me witness, that I said, 'I am not the Christ, but I have been sent before him.' The one who has the bride is the bridegroom. The friend of the bridegroom, who stands and hears him, rejoices greatly at the bridegroom's voice. Therefore this joy of mine is now complete. He must increase, but I must decrease."

He who comes from above is above all. He who is of the earth belongs to the earth and speaks in an earthly way. He who comes from heaven is above all. He bears witness to what he has seen and heard, yet no one receives his testimony. Whoever receives his testimony sets his seal to this, that God is true. For he whom God has sent speaks[4] the words of God, for he gives the Spirit without measure. The Father loves the Son and has given all things into his hand. Whoever believes in the Son has eternal life; whoever does not obey the Son shall not see life, but the wrath of God remains on him.

Now when Jesus learned that the Pharisees had heard that Jesus was making and baptizing more disciples than John (although Jesus himself did not baptize, but only his disciples), he left Judea and departed again for Galilee.

---

[4] ESV reads: utters the words of God,

31

Session 4

1.1   Who believed Jesus was a teacher who has come from God?

1.2   Why did they believe this?

2.0   What did Jesus say must happen in order for someone to see the kingdom of God?

3.0   What do you think Jesus is referring to when He speaks of "water" in John 3:5? (Note: the entire phrase "born of water and the Spirit" refers to the spiritual birth. You may also want to refer to the cross-reference of the phrase "of water and spirit" in v. 5 and the ESV Study Bible Notes on John 3:3-6.)

4.1   In Numbers 21:6-9, why did the Lord send venomous serpents amongst the Israelites?

4.2   What must someone who has been bitten do in order to live?

4.3   What was it about this action that allowed the bitten individual to live?

4.4   How does this biblical account relate to Jesus (John 3:14-15)?

5.0   What motivated God that "He gave His only (i.e. unique, one-of-a-kind) Son?"

additional notes

Session 4

6.0 Why do evil people hate Jesus Christ?

7.0 True or False: Jesus Christ personally baptized people with water? ☐ True ☐ False

8.1 What "discussion arose" between John's disciples and a Jew?

8.2 In John 3:29, who are: the bride, the groom, and the friend?

8.3 And what did John say "must" happen in contrasting him and Jesus?

9.1 What does one do who receives Jesus' "testimony" (i.e. that He is from above and bears witness to what He has seen and heard)?

9.2 What does this mean (Note: you may want to refer to the ESV Study Bible Notes and reference)?

9.3 With what kind of words does Jesus speak (i.e. "utter")?

10.1 Who has "eternal life" (Note: you may want to refer to the ESV Study Bible Notes)?

10.2 What remains on the person who "does not obey the Son?"

additional notes

Session 5

And he had to pass through Samaria. So he came to a town of Samaria called Sychar, near the field that Jacob had given to his son Joseph. Jacob's well was there; so Jesus, tired[5] as he was from his journey, was sitting beside the well. It was about the sixth hour.

A woman from Samaria came to draw water. Jesus said to her, "Give me a drink." (For his disciples had gone away into the city to buy food.) The Samaritan woman said to him, "How is it that you, a Jew, ask for a drink from me, a woman of Samaria?" (For Jews have no dealings with Samaritans.) Jesus answered her, "If you knew the gift of God, and who it is that is saying to you, 'Give me a drink,' you would have asked him, and he would have given you living water." The woman said to him, "Sir, you have nothing to draw water with, and the well is deep. Where do you get that living water? Are you greater than our father Jacob? He gave us the well and drank from it himself, as did his sons and his livestock." Jesus said to her, "Everyone who drinks of this water will be thirsty again, but whoever drinks of the water that I will give him will never be thirsty again. The water that I will give him will become in him a spring of water welling up to eternal life." The woman said to him, "Sir, give me this water, so that I will not be thirsty or have to come here to draw water."

Jesus said to her, "Go, call your husband, and come here." The woman answered him, "I have no husband." Jesus said to her, "You are right in saying, 'I have no husband'; for you have had five husbands, and the one you now have is not your husband. What you have said is true." The woman said to him, "Sir, I perceive that you are a prophet. Our fathers worshiped on this mountain, but you say that in Jerusalem is the place where people ought to worship." Jesus said to her, "Woman, believe me, the hour is coming when neither on this mountain nor in Jerusalem will you worship the Father. You worship what you do not know; we worship what we know, for salvation is from the Jews. But the hour is coming, and is now here,

---

[5] ESV reads: "wearied" as he was from his journey,

when the true worshipers will worship the Father in spirit and truth, for the Father is seeking such people to worship him. God is spirit, and those who worship him must worship in spirit and truth." The woman said to him, "I know that Messiah is coming (he who is called Christ). When he comes, he will tell us all things." Jesus said to her, "I who speak to you am he."

Just then his disciples came back. They marveled that he was talking with a woman, but no one said, "What do you seek?" or, "Why are you talking with her?" So the woman left her water jar and went away into town and said to the people, "Come, see a man who told me all that I ever did. Can this be the Christ?" They went out of the town and were coming to him.

Meanwhile the disciples were urging him, saying, "Rabbi, eat." But he said to them, "I have food to eat that you do not know about." So the disciples said to one another, "Has anyone brought him something to eat?" Jesus said to them, "My food is to do the will of him who sent me and to accomplish his work. Do you not say, 'There are yet four months, then comes the harvest'? Look, I tell you, lift up your eyes, and see that the fields are white for harvest. Already the one who reaps is receiving wages and gathering fruit for eternal life, so that sower and reaper may rejoice together. For here the saying holds true, 'One sows and another reaps.' I sent you to reap that for which you did not labor. Others have labored, and you have entered into their labor."

Many Samaritans from that town believed in him because of the woman's testimony, "He told me all that I ever did." So when the Samaritans came to him, they asked him to stay with them, and he stayed there two days. And many more believed because of his word. They said to the woman, "It is no longer because of what you said that we believe, for we have heard for ourselves, and we know that this is indeed the Savior of the world."

John 4:4-54

After the two days he departed for Galilee. (For Jesus himself had testified that a prophet has no honor in his own hometown.) So when he came to Galilee, the Galileans welcomed him, having seen all that he had done in Jerusalem at the feast. For they too had gone to the feast.

So he came again to Cana in Galilee, where he had made the water wine. And at Capernaum there was an official whose son was ill. When this man heard that Jesus had come from Judea to Galilee, he went to him and begged him to come down and heal his son, for he was at the point of death.[6] So Jesus said to him, "Unless you see signs and wonders you will not believe." The official said to him, "Sir, come down before my child dies." Jesus said to him, "Go; your son will live." The man believed the word that Jesus spoke to him and went on his way. As he was going down, his servants met him and told him that his son was recovering. So he asked them the hour when he began to get better, and they said to him, "Yesterday at the seventh hour the fever left him." The father knew that was the hour when Jesus had said to him, "Your son will live." And he himself believed, and all his household. This was now the second sign that Jesus did when he had come from Judea to Galilee.

---

[6] ESV reads, "When this man heard that Jesus had come from Judea to Galilee, he went to him and asked him to come down and heal his son, for he was at the point of death."

additional notes

Session 5

1.1   Why did Jesus sit down beside Jacob's well?

1.2   What time (present day time) was it when He sat down by the well?

2.0   What do you think Jesus may have looked, talked, and/or acted like according to John 4:7-9? Explain.

3.0   According to John 4:10-15 with John 7:38-39, what is the "living water" (note: you may want to refer to the cross-reference and ESV Study Bible Notes concerning this "living water")?

4.1   Once the Samaritan woman realized Jesus was a prophet, what probing topic did she want to talk about?

4.2   What was Jesus' response?

5.1   Who did Jesus claim to be in John 4:25-26?

5.2   How did the Samaritan woman respond to this claim?

additional notes

Session 5

6. 0 In John 4:27-38, what do you think Jesus means when He refers to each of the following: food, fields, sower, and reaper?

7.1 Initially, why did "many Samaritans from that town" believe Jesus was the Christ?

7.2 After Jesus had stayed with the Samaritans two days, why did many more Samaritans believe?

8.1 **How far did the official travel to find Jesus** (note: you may want to refer to the map titled, "Jesus' Ministry in Galilee" located in the ESV Study Bible Notes)**?**

8.2 **In what manner did the official ask Jesus to come and heal his son** (note: you may want to refer to the provided translation in your workbook to help better answer this question)**?**

9.1 How did the official respond when Jesus said, "Go; your son will live?"

9.2 What time (present day time) was it when Jesus said this?

9.3 What question did the official ask when he met his servant and what was the result of the servant's answer?

additional notes

Session 6

John 5:1-47

After this there was a feast of the Jews, and Jesus went up to Jerusalem.

Now there is in Jerusalem by the Sheep Gate a pool, in Aramaic called Bethesda, which has five roofed colonnades. In these lay a multitude of invalids—blind, lame, and paralyzed. One man was there who had been an invalid for thirty-eight years. When Jesus saw him lying there and knew that he had already been there a long time, he said to him, "Do you want to be healed?" The sick man answered him, "Sir, I have no one to put me into the pool when the water is stirred up, and while I am going another steps down before me." Jesus said to him, "Get up, take up your bed, and walk." And at once the man was healed, and he took up his bed and walked.

Now that day was the Sabbath. So the Jews said to the man who had been healed, "It is the Sabbath, and it is not lawful for you to take up your bed." But he answered them, "The man who healed me, that man said to me, 'Take up your bed, and walk.'" They asked him, "Who is the man who said to you, 'Take up your bed and walk'?" Now the man who had been healed did not know who it was, for Jesus had withdrawn, as there was a crowd in the place. Afterward Jesus found him in the temple and said to him, "See, you are well! Sin no more, that nothing worse may happen to you." The man went away and told the Jews that it was Jesus who had healed him. And this was why the Jews were persecuting Jesus, because he was doing these things on the Sabbath. But Jesus answered them, "My Father is working until now, and I am working."

This was why the Jews were seeking all the more to kill him, because not only was he breaking the Sabbath, but he was even calling God his own Father, making himself equal with God.

So Jesus said to them, "Truly, truly, I say to you, the Son can do nothing of his own accord, but only what he sees the Father doing. For whatever the Father does, that the Son does likewise. For the Father loves the Son and shows him all that he himself is doing. And

greater works than these will he show him, so that you may marvel. For as the Father raises the dead and gives them life, so also the Son gives life to whom he will. The Father judges no one, but has given all judgment to the Son, that all may honor the Son, just as they honor the Father. Whoever does not honor the Son does not honor the Father who sent him. Truly, truly, I say to you, whoever hears my word and believes him who sent me has eternal life. He does not come into judgment, but has passed from death to life.

"Truly, truly, I say to you, an hour is coming, and is now here, when the dead will hear the voice of the Son of God, and those who hear will live. For as the Father has life in himself, so he has granted the Son also to have life in himself. And he has given him authority to execute judgment, because he is the Son of Man. Do not marvel at this, for an hour is coming when all who are in the tombs will hear his voice and come out, those who have done good to the resurrection of life, and those who have done evil to the resurrection of judgment.

"I can do nothing on my own. As I hear, I judge, and my judgment is just, because I seek not my own will but the will of him who sent me. If I alone bear witness about myself, my testimony is not true. There is another who bears witness about me, and I know that the testimony that he bears about me is true. You sent to John, and he has borne witness to the truth. Not that the testimony that I receive is from man, but I say these things so that you may be saved. He was a burning and shining lamp, and you were willing to rejoice for a while in his light. But the testimony that I have is greater than that of John. For the works that the Father has given me to accomplish, the very works that I am doing, bear witness about me that the Father has sent me. And the Father who sent me has himself borne witness about me. His voice you have never heard, his form you have never seen, and you do not have his word abiding in you, for you do not believe the one whom he has sent. You search the Scriptures because you think that in them you have eternal life; and it

is they that bear witness about me, yet you refuse to come to me that you may have life. I do not receive glory from people. But I know that you do not have the love of God within you. I have come in my Father's name, and you do not receive me. If another comes in his own name, you will receive him. How can you believe, when you receive glory from one another and do not seek the glory that comes from the only God? Do not think that I will accuse you to the Father. There is one who accuses you: Moses, on whom you have set your hope. For if you believed Moses, you would believe me; for he wrote of me. But if you do not believe his writings, how will you believe my words?

additional notes

Session 6

1.1   **How long had the invalid been in his condition?**

1.2   **How do you think the invalid was hoping to be cured?**

1.3   **What did the invalid believe he needed in order to be healed in this manner?**

2.1   **What does John 5:4 state** (hint: you may want to refer to ESV footnote and ESV Study Bible Notes on John 5:3)**?**

2.2   **How do you explain that this supposed verse was originally included in the numbering of scripture?**

3.0   **Why do you think Jesus asked the invalid, "Do you want to be healed?"**

4.0   **What correlation do you see between the invalid's faith in Christ and his healing? Explain** (hint: you may want to consider what the invalid was trusting in for his healing)**.**

5.0   **What do you think Jesus meant by his statement(s) in verse 14** (hint: you may want to consider what the invalid did as soon as Jesus told him to stop sinning)**?**

additional notes

Session 6

6.1   Explain why "the Jews were persecuting Jesus."

6.2   Why did they try "all the more to kill Him?"

7.1   What does Jesus do on His own?

7.2   How much of what the Father does is shown to the Son?

7.3   Why does the Father show the Son these things?

8.1   What are at least two things that the Father does/has that He has the Son do/give/have?

8.2   Why has the Father allowed or given these things to the Son?

9.1   What must someone do in order to have "eternal life"?

9.2   Considering the context of this passage (i.e. v. 24), what do you think is meant by "good" and "evil" in verse 29?

10.0 List at least four people or things that "bear witness" to Jesus in John 5:30-46 (hint: you may want to look at the chart, "Witnesses to Jesus" in the ESV Study Notes for some additional help).

additional notes

Session 7

Matt. 14:13-36	Mark 6:30-56	Luke 9:10-17	John 6:1-24
Now when Jesus heard this, he withdrew from there in a boat to a desolate place by himself. But when the crowds heard it, they followed him on foot from the towns. When he went ashore he saw a great crowd, and he had compassion on them and healed their sick. Now when it was evening, the disciples came to him and said, "This is a desolate place, and the day is now over; send the crowds away to go into the villages and buy food for themselves." But Jesus said, "They need not go away; you give them something to eat." They said to him, "We have only five loaves here and two fish." And he said,	The apostles returned to Jesus and told him all that they had done and taught. And he said to them, "Come away by yourselves to a desolate place and rest a while." For many were coming and going, and they had no leisure even to eat. And they went away in the boat to a desolate place by themselves. Now many saw them going and recognized them, and they ran there on foot from all the towns and got there ahead of them. When he went ashore he saw a great crowd, and he had compassion on them, because they were like sheep without a shepherd. And he began to teach	On their return the apostles told him all that they had done. And he took them and withdrew apart to a town called Bethsaida. When the crowds learned it, they followed him, and he welcomed them and spoke to them of the kingdom of God and cured those who had need of healing. Now the day began to wear away, and the twelve came and said to him, "Send the crowd away to go into the surrounding villages and countryside to find lodging and get provisions, for we are here in a desolate place." But he "You give them something to eat." They said, "We have no more than five loaves and two fish—unless we	After this Jesus went away to the other side of the Sea of Galilee, which is the Sea of Tiberias. And a large crowd was following him, because they saw the signs that he was doing on the sick. Jesus went up on the mountain, and there he sat down with his disciples. Now the Passover, the feast of the Jews, was at hand. Lifting up his eyes, then, and seeing that a large crowd was coming toward him, Jesus said to Philip, "Where are we to buy bread, so that these people may eat?" He said this to test him, for he himself knew what he would do. Philip answered him, "Two hundred denarii worth of bread would not

52

Matt. 14:13-36	Mark 6:30-56	Luke 9:10-17	John 6:1-24
"Bring them here to me." Then he ordered the crowds to sit down on the grass, and taking the five loaves and the two fish, he looked up to heaven and said a blessing. Then he broke the loaves and gave them to the disciples, and the disciples gave them to the crowds. And they all ate and were satisfied. And they took up twelve baskets full of the broken pieces left over. And those who ate were about five thousand men, besides women and children.

Immediately he made the disciples get into the boat and go before him to the other side, while he dismissed the crowds. And after | them many things. And when it grew late, his disciples came to him and said, "This is a desolate place, and the hour is now late. Send them away to go into the surrounding countryside and villages and buy themselves something to eat." But he answered them, "You give them something to eat." And they said to him, "Shall we go and buy two hundred denarii worth of bread and give it to them to eat?" And he said to them, "How many loaves do you have? Go and see." And when they had found out, they said, "Five, and two fish." Then he commanded them all to sit down in groups | are to go and buy food for all these people."
For there were about five thousand men. And he said to his disciples, "Have them sit down in groups of about fifty each." And they did so, and had them all sit down. And taking the five loaves and the two fish, he looked up to heaven and said a blessing over them. Then he broke the loaves and gave them to the disciples to set before the crowd. And they all ate and were satisfied. And what was left over was picked up, twelve baskets of broken pieces. | be enough for each of them to get a little." One of his disciples, Andrew, Simon Peter's brother, said to him, "There is a boy here who has five barley loaves and two fish, but what are they for so many?" Jesus said, "Have the people sit down." Now there was much grass in the place. So the men sat down, about five thousand in number. Jesus then took the loaves, and when he had given thanks, he distributed them to those who were seated. So also the fish, as much as they wanted. And when they had eaten their fill, he told his disciples, "Gather up the leftover fragments, that nothing may be lost." So they |

Matt. 14:13-36	Mark 6:30-56	John 6:1-24
he had dismissed the crowds, he went up on the mountain by himself to pray. When evening came, he was there alone, but the boat by this time was a long way from the land, beaten by the waves, for the wind was against them. And in the fourth watch of the night he came to them, walking on the sea. But when the disciples saw him walking on the sea, they were terrified, and said, "It is a ghost!" and they cried out in fear. But immediately Jesus spoke to them, saying, "Take heart; it is I. Do not be afraid." And Peter answered him, "Lord, if it is you, command me to come to you on the water." He said, "Come." So Peter got out of	on the green grass. So they sat down in groups, by hundreds and by fifties. And taking the five loaves and the two fish he looked up to heaven and said a blessing and broke the loaves and gave them to the disciples to set before the people. And he divided the two fish among them all. And they all ate and were satisfied. And they took up twelve baskets full of broken pieces and of the fish. And those who ate the loaves were five thousand men. Immediately he made his disciples get into the boat and go before him to the other side, to Bethsaida, while he dismissed the crowd. And after he had taken	gathered them up and filled twelve baskets with fragments from the five barley loaves left by those who had eaten. When the people saw the sign that he had done, they said, "This is indeed the Prophet who is to come into the world!" Perceiving then that they were about to come and take him by force to make him king, Jesus withdrew again to the mountain by himself. When evening came, his disciples went down to the sea, got into a boat, and started across the sea to Capernaum. It was now dark, and Jesus had not yet come to them. The sea became rough because a strong wind was blowing. When they had rowed

Matt. 14:13-36	Mark 6:30-56	John 6:1-24
the boat and walked on the water and came to Jesus. But when he saw the wind, he was afraid, and beginning to sink he cried out, "Lord, save me." Jesus immediately reached out his hand and took hold of him, saying to him, "O you of little faith, why did you doubt?" And when they got into the boat, the wind ceased. And those in the boat worshiped him, saying, "Truly you are the Son of God." And when they had crossed over, they came to land at Gennesaret. And when the men of that place recognized him, they sent around to all that region and brought to him all who were	leave of them, he went up on the mountain to pray. And when evening came, the boat was out on the sea, and he was alone on the land. And he saw that they were making headway painfully, for the wind was against them. And about the fourth watch of the night he came to them, walking on the sea. He meant to pass by them, but when they saw him walking on the sea they thought it was a ghost, and cried out, for they all saw him and were terrified. But immediately he spoke to them and said, "Take heart; it is I. Do not be afraid." And he got into the boat with them, and the wind ceased. And they were utterly	about three or four miles, they saw Jesus walking on the sea and coming near the boat, and they were frightened. But he said to them, "It is I; do not be afraid." Then they were glad to take him into the boat, and immediately the boat was at the land to which they were going. On the next day the crowd that remained on the other side of the sea saw that there had been only one boat there, and that Jesus had not entered the boat with his disciples, but that his disciples had gone away alone. Other boats from Tiberias came near the place where they had eaten the bread after the Lord had given thanks. So

55

Matt. 14:13-36	Mark 6:30-56		John 6:1-24
sick and implored him that they might only touch the fringe of his garment. And as many as touched it were made well.	astounded, for they did not understand about the loaves, but their hearts were hardened. When they had crossed over, they came to land at Gennesaret and moored to the shore. And when they got out of the boat, the people immediately recognized him and ran about the whole region and began to bring the sick people on their beds to wherever they heard he was. And wherever he came, in villages, cities, or countryside, they laid the sick in the marketplaces and implored him that they might touch even the garment. And as many as touched it were made well.		when the crowd saw that Jesus was not there, nor his disciples, they themselves got into the boats and went to Capernaum, seeking Jesus.

John 6:25-71

When they found him on the other side of the sea, they said to him, "Rabbi, when did you come here?" Jesus answered them, "Truly, truly, I say to you, you are seeking me, not because you saw signs, but because you ate your fill of the loaves. Do not work for the food that perishes, but for the food that endures to eternal life, which the Son of Man will give to you. For on him God the Father has set his seal." Then they said to him, "What must we do, to be doing the works of God?" Jesus answered them, "This is the work of God, that you believe in him whom he has sent." So they said to him, "Then what sign do you do, that we may see and believe you? What work do you perform? Our fathers ate the manna in the wilderness; as it is written, 'He gave them bread from heaven to eat.'" Jesus then said to them, "Truly, truly, I say to you, it was not Moses who gave you the bread from heaven, but my Father gives you the true bread from heaven. For the bread of God is he who comes down from heaven and gives life to the world." They said to him, "Sir, give us this bread always."

Jesus said to them, "I am the bread of life; whoever comes to me shall not hunger, and whoever believes in me shall never thirst. But I said to you that you have seen me and yet do not believe. All that the Father gives me will come to me, and whoever comes to me I will never cast out. For I have come down from heaven, not to do my own will but the will of him who sent me. And this is the will of him who sent me, that I should lose nothing of all that he has given me, but raise it up on the last day. For this is the will of my Father, that everyone who looks on the Son and believes in him should have eternal life, and I will raise him up on the last day."

So the Jews grumbled about him, because he said, "I am the bread that came down from heaven." They said, "Is not this Jesus, the son of Joseph, whose father and mother we know? How does he now say, 'I have come down from heaven'?" Jesus answered them, "Do not grumble among yourselves. No one can come to me unless the Father who sent me draws him. And I will raise him up on the last

day. It is written in the Prophets, 'And they will all be taught by God.' Everyone who has heard and learned from the Father comes to me—not that anyone has seen the Father except he who is from God; he has seen the Father. Truly, truly, I say to you, whoever believes has eternal life. I am the bread of life. Your fathers ate the manna in the wilderness, and they died. This is the bread that comes down from heaven, so that one may eat of it and not die. I am the living bread that came down from heaven. If anyone eats of this bread, he will live forever. And the bread that I will give for the life of the world is my flesh."

The Jews then disputed among themselves, saying, "How can this man give us his flesh to eat?" So Jesus said to them, "Truly, truly, I say to you, unless you eat the flesh of the Son of Man and drink his blood, you have no life in you. Whoever feeds on my flesh and drinks my blood has eternal life, and I will raise him up on the last day. For my flesh is true food, and my blood is true drink. Whoever feeds on my flesh and drinks my blood lives in me, and I in him. As the living Father sent me, and I live because of the Father, so whoever feeds on me, he also will live because of me. This is the bread that came down from heaven, not like the bread the fathers ate, and died. Whoever feeds on this bread will live forever." Jesus said these things in the synagogue, as he taught at Capernaum.

When many of his disciples heard it, they said, "This is a hard saying; who can listen to it?" But Jesus, knowing in himself that his disciples were grumbling about this, said to them, "Do you take offense at this? Then what if you were to see the Son of Man ascending to where he was before? It is the Spirit who gives life; the flesh is no help at all.

The words that I have spoken to you are spirit and life. But there are some of you who do not believe." (For Jesus knew from the beginning who those were who did not believe, and who it was who would betray him.) And he said, "This is why I told you that no one

can come to me unless it is granted him by the Father."

After this many of his disciples turned back and no longer walked with him. So Jesus said to the Twelve, "Do you want to go away as well?" Simon Peter answered him, "Lord, to whom shall we go? You have the words of eternal life, and we have believed, and have come to know, that you are the Holy One of God." Jesus answered them, "Did I not choose you, the Twelve? And yet one of you is a devil." He spoke of Judas the son of Simon Iscariot, for he, one of the Twelve, was going to betray him.

Session 7

Short Answer: Matthew 14:13-36; Mark 6:30-56; Luke 9:10-17; John 6:1-24. Write the reference (chapter and verse) that best supports your answer (note: all questions and quotes are taken from the ESV translation).

1.1   What did Jesus do right before He broke bread and gave it to the people?

1.2   Why do you think He did this?

2.1   About how many total people do you think were fed (hint: you may want to refer to the ESV Study Bible Notes)?

2.2   Roughly how many groups would there be (assuming about half of the groups had a hundred people and the other half had fifty)?

2.3   How much did the disciples say it would cost to feed all these people?

3.1   How many total baskets of leftovers did the twelve disciples gather?

3.2   What are some things you think the feeding the multitude should have taught the Disciples about God?

additional notes

Session 7

4.1   When Peter saw Jesus walking on the water, what did he ask the Lord to do in order to show that it was truly Jesus?

4.2   About what time (present day time) was it when the disciples set sail?

4.3   About what time (present day time) was it when Jesus went out to the disciples on the lake?

4.4   About how far had the disciples traveled before they saw Jesus walking on the lake?

4.5   About how long did it take them to get that far?

4.6   About how far was it from where the disciples had set sail on the lake to where they eventually arrived (note: you may want to refer to a map in a Bible Atlas)?

4.7   What did the disciples do when Peter and Jesus climbed into the boat and the wind died down?

4.8   How long did it take the disciples to reach the shore after they had taken Jesus into the boat?

4.9   In Mark 6:51-52, why were the disciples "utterly astounded" when the winds ceased? What do you think this means?

additional notes

Session 7

Short Answer: John 6:25-71 and Exodus 16:1-36. Write the reference (chapter and verse) that best supports your answer (note: all questions and quotes are taken from the ESV translation).

5.1   What kind of "food" did Jesus say people should "work" for?

5.2   How does Jesus define, "The work of God?"

6.1   How do you think the Jews would define the "bread of God?"

6.2   How does Jesus define, "bread of God?"

7.1   What did Jesus claim in John 6:35?

7.2   How did the Jews respond to Jesus' claims?

8.0   What is the only way in which someone can "come" to Jesus?

9.1   How did Peter respond when Jesus asked the disciples, "Do you want to go away as well?"

9.2   Is this how you would have expected the disciples to answer this question (i.e. is this how you would have responded)? **Explain.**

additional notes

John 7:1 – 8:59

After this Jesus went about in Galilee. He would not go about in Judea, because the Jews were seeking to kill him. Now the Jews' Feast of Booths was at hand. So his brothers said to him, "Leave here and go to Judea, that your disciples also may see the works you are doing. For no one works in secret if he seeks to be known openly. If you do these things, show yourself to the world." For not even his brothers believed in him. Jesus said to them, "My time has not yet[7] come, but your time is always here. The world cannot hate you, but it hates me because I testify about it that its works are evil. You go up to the feast. I am not yet going up to this feast, for my time has not yet fully come." After saying this, he remained in Galilee.

But after his brothers had gone up to the feast, then he also went up, not publicly but in private. The Jews were looking for him at the feast, and saying, "Where is he?" And there was much muttering about him among the people. While some said, "He is a good man," others said, "No, he is leading the people astray." Yet for fear of the Jews no one spoke openly of him.

About the middle of the feast Jesus went up into the temple and began teaching. The Jews therefore marveled, saying, "How is it that this man has learning, when he has never studied?" So Jesus answered them, "My teaching is not mine, but his who sent me. If anyone's will is to do God's will, he will know whether the teaching is from God or whether I am speaking on my own authority. The one who speaks on his own authority seeks his own glory; but the one who seeks the glory of him who sent him is true, and in him there is no falsehood. Has not Moses given you the law? Yet none of you keeps the law. Why do you seek to kill me?" The crowd answered, "You have a demon! Who is seeking to kill you?" Jesus answered them, "I did one work, and you all marvel at it. Moses gave you circumcision (not that it is from Moses, but from the fathers), and you circumcise a man on the Sabbath. If on the Sabbath a man receives

---

[7] Some manuscripts add yet

circumcision, so that the law of Moses may not be broken, are you angry with me because on the Sabbath I made a man's whole body well? Do not judge by appearances, but judge with right judgment."

Some of the people of Jerusalem therefore said, "Is not this the man whom they seek to kill? And here he is, speaking openly, and they say nothing to him! Can it be that the authorities really know that this is the Christ? But we know where this man comes from, and when the Christ appears, no one will know where he comes from." So Jesus proclaimed, as he taught in the temple, "You know me, and you know where I come from. But I have not come of my own accord. He who sent me is true, and him you do not know. I know him, for I come from him, and he sent me." So they were seeking to arrest him, but no one laid a hand on him, because his hour had not yet come. Yet many of the people believed in him. They said, "When the Christ appears, will he do more signs than this man has done?"

The Pharisees heard the crowd muttering these things about him, and the chief priests and Pharisees sent officers to arrest him. Jesus then said, "I will be with you a little longer, and then I am going to him who sent me. You will seek me and you will not find me. Where I am you cannot come." The Jews said to one another, "Where does this man intend to go that we will not find him? Does he intend to go to the Dispersion among the Greeks and teach the Greeks? What does he mean by saying, 'You will seek me and you will not find me,' and, 'Where I am you cannot come'?"
On the last day of the feast, the great day, Jesus stood up and cried out, "If anyone thirsts, let him come to me and drink. Whoever believes in me, as the Scripture has said, 'Out of his heart will flow rivers of living water.'" Now this he said about the Spirit, whom those who believed in him were to receive, for as yet the Spirit had not been given, because Jesus was not yet glorified.

When they heard these words, some of the people said, "This really is the Prophet." Others said, "This is the Christ." But some said,

John 7:1 – 8:59

"Is the Christ to come from Galilee? Has not the Scripture said that the Christ comes from the offspring of David, and comes from Bethlehem, the village where David was?" So there was a division among the people over him. Some of them wanted to arrest him, but no one laid hands on him.

The officers then came to the chief priests and Pharisees, who said to them, "Why did you not bring him?" The officers answered, "No one ever spoke like this man!" The Pharisees answered them, "Have you also been deceived? Have any of the authorities or the Pharisees believed in him? But this crowd that does not know the law is accursed." Nicodemus, who had gone to him before, and who was one of them, said to them, "Does our law judge a man without first giving him a hearing and learning what he does?" They replied, "Are you from Galilee too? Search and see that no prophet arises from Galilee."

[They went each to his own house, but Jesus went to the Mount of Olives. Early in the morning he came again to the temple. All the people came to him, and he sat down and taught them. The scribes and the Pharisees brought a woman who had been caught in adultery, and placing her in the midst they said to him, "Teacher, this woman has been caught in the act of adultery. Now in the Law Moses commanded us to stone such women. So what do you say?" This they said to test him, that they might have some charge to bring against him. Jesus bent down and wrote with his finger on the ground. And as they continued to ask him, he stood up and said to them, "Let him who is without sin among you be the first to throw a stone at her." And once more he bent down and wrote on the ground. But when they heard it, they went away one by one, beginning with the older ones, and Jesus was left alone with the woman standing before him. Jesus stood up and said to her, "Woman, where are they? Has no one condemned you?" She said, "No one, Lord." And Jesus said, "Neither do I condemn you; go, and from now on sin no more."]

John 7:1 – 8:59

Again Jesus spoke to them, saying, "I am the light of the world. Whoever follows me will not walk in darkness, but will have the light of life." So the Pharisees said to him, "You are bearing witness about yourself; your testimony is not true." Jesus answered, "Even if I do bear witness about myself, my testimony is true, for I know where I came from and where I am going, but you do not know where I come from or where I am going. You judge according to the flesh; I judge no one. Yet even if I do judge, my judgment is true, for it is not I alone who judge, but I and the Father who sent me. In your Law it is written that the testimony of two people is true. I am the one who bears witness about myself, and the Father who sent me bears witness about me." They said to him therefore, "Where is your Father?" Jesus answered, "You know neither me nor my Father. If you knew me, you would know my Father also." These words he spoke in the treasury, as he taught in the temple; but no one arrested him, because his hour had not yet come.

So he said to them again, "I am going away, and you will seek me, and you will die in your sin. Where I am going, you cannot come." So the Jews said, "Will he kill himself, since he says, 'Where I am going, you cannot come'?" He said to them, "You are from below; I am from above. You are of this world; I am not of this world. I told you that you would die in your sins, for unless you believe that I am you will die in your sins." So they said to him, "Who are you?" Jesus said to them, "Just what I have been telling you from the beginning. I have much to say about you and much to judge, but he who sent me is true, and I declare to the world what I have heard from him." They did not understand that he had been speaking to them about the Father. So Jesus said to them, "When you have lifted up the Son of Man, then you will know that I am, and that I do nothing on my own authority, but speak just as the Father taught me. And he who sent me is with me. He has not left me alone, for I always do the things

that are pleasing to him." As he was saying these things, many believed in him.

So Jesus said to the Jews who had believed him, "If you live in my word, you are truly my disciples, and you will know the truth, and the truth will set you free." They answered him, "We are offspring of Abraham and have never been enslaved to anyone. How is it that you say, 'You will become free'?"

Jesus answered them, "Truly, truly, I say to you, everyone who practices sin is a slave to sin. Now a slave does not live in the family forever; the son lives in the family forever.[8] So if the Son sets you free, you will be free indeed. I know that you are offspring of Abraham; yet you seek to kill me because my word finds no place in you. I speak of what I have seen with my Father, and you do what you have heard from your father."

They answered him, "Abraham is our father." Jesus said to them, "If you were Abraham's children, you would be doing the works Abraham did, but now you seek to kill me, a man who has told you the truth that I heard from God. This is not what Abraham did. You are doing the works your father did." They said to him, "We were not born of sexual immorality. We have one Father—even God." Jesus said to them, "If God were your Father, you would love me, for I came from God and I am here. I came not of my own accord, but he sent me. Why do you not understand what I say? It is because you cannot bear to hear my word. You are of your father the devil, and your will is to do your father's desires. He was a murderer from the beginning, and does not stand in the truth, because there is no truth in him. When he lies, he speaks out of his own character, for he is a liar and the father of lies. But because I tell the truth, you do not believe me. Which one of you convicts me of sin? If I tell the truth, why do you

---

[8] The ESV states, "The slave does not remain in the house forever; the son remains forever."

70

John 7:1 – 8:59

not believe me? Whoever is of God hears the words of God. The reason why you do not hear them is that you are not of God."

The Jews answered him, "Are we not right in saying that you are a Samaritan and have a demon?" Jesus answered, "I do not have a demon, but I honor my Father, and you dishonor me. Yet I do not seek my own glory; there is One who seeks it, and he is the judge. Truly, truly, I say to you, if anyone keeps my word, he will never see death." The Jews said to him, "Now we know that you have a demon! Abraham died, as did the prophets, yet you say, 'If anyone keeps my word, he will never taste death.' Are you greater than our father Abraham, who died? And the prophets died! Who do you make yourself out to be?" Jesus answered, "If I glorify myself, my glory is nothing. It is my Father who glorifies me, of whom you say, 'He is our God.' But you have not known him. I know him. If I were to say that I do not know him, I would be a liar like you, but I do know him and I keep his word. Your father Abraham rejoiced that he would see my day. He saw it and was glad." So the Jews said to him, "You are not yet fifty years old, and have you seen Abraham?" Jesus said to them, "Truly, truly, I say to you, before Abraham was, I AM." So they picked up stones to throw at him, but Jesus hid himself and went out of the temple.

Session 8

1.1 **What is the Feast of Booths** (note: you may want to cross-reference "Feasts of Booths" in John 7:2 and also read the ESV Study Bible Notes associated with this reference)**?**

1.2 **Why did Jesus go to Judea in "secret?"**

1.3 **Why didn't anyone lay a hand on Him when they tried to seize Him in John 7:30 and 8:20?**

2.1 **Where did Jesus receive His doctrine (i.e. teaching)?**

2.2 **How could someone know whether Jesus' teaching comes from God?**

2.3 **What did the Jews believe God's will was for their lives** (John 7:19)**?**

2.4 **Were the Jews living up to their own standard of doing God's will?**

2.5 **How did Jesus say the Jews should judge?**

3.1 **How does John 7:1 - 8:59 support Jesus' statement in John 7:19, even though the people denied it in John 7:20?**

3.2 **What made some of the people from Jerusalem conclude that the Jewish authorities might have thought Jesus was the Christ?**

3.3 **What is meant by "the Dispersion among the Greeks" and where else is this referenced in the NT and OT** (hint: you may want to cross-reference this phrase)**?**

additional notes

Session 8

4.0 **Why did some of the Jews believe the Messiah must come from Bethlehem** (note: you may want to cross-reference "Bethlehem" and also read the ESV Study Bible Notes associated with these various references)**?**

5.1 **What was the qualification for throwing the first stone at the adulterous woman?**

5.2 **Did anyone meet this qualification?**

5.3 **What do you think Jesus bent down and wrote on the ground?**

5.4 **Why do you think the older men were the first to leave?**

6.1 **Where is it written in the Law** (i.e. Old Testament) **that the testimony of two witnesses is valid** (hint: you may want to refer to the cross-references in John 8:17. Note: whenever cross-references to specific words or phrases appear as "See" it denotes less direct references.)**?**

6.2 **When explaining about the validity of His testimony, why did Jesus say that the Pharisees did not know His Father?**

7.0 **What did Jesus say could not happen, as well as what would happen, to someone "unless you believe that I am?"**

additional notes

Session 8

8.1   Who are "truly [Jesus'] disciples" (note: you may want to refer to the provided translation in your workbook to help better answer this question)?

8.2   What will Jesus' true disciples know and what will this do for them?

9.1   Who is a slave to sin?

9.2   How long does a slave live in the family (note: you may want to refer to the provided translation in your workbook to help better answer this question)?

9.3   How long does a son live in the family (note: you may want to refer to the provided translation in your workbook to help better answer this question)?

10.1   What did Jesus say the Jews would be doing if they were "Abraham's children"?

10.2   What did Jesus say the Jews would do if they were children of God?

10.3   Who did Jesus say was the Pharisee's father?

11.0   Who "will never see/taste death"?

12.0   What did Jesus say that prompted the Jews to pick up stones and try to stone Him?

additional notes

John 9:1 – 10:42

As he passed by, he saw a man blind from birth. And his disciples asked him, "Rabbi, who sinned, this man or his parents, that he was born blind?" Jesus answered, "It was not that this man sinned, or his parents, but that the works of God might be displayed in him. We must work the works of him who sent me while it is day; night is coming, when no one can work. As long as I am in the world, I am the light of the world." Having said these things, he spit on the ground and made mud with the saliva. Then he anointed the man's eyes with the mud and said to him, "Go, wash in the pool of Siloam" (which means Sent). So he went and washed and came back seeing.

The neighbors and those who had seen him before as a beggar were saying, "Is this not the man who used to sit and beg?" Some said, "It is he." Others said, "No, but he is like him." He kept saying, "I am the man." So they said to him, "Then how were your eyes opened?" He answered, "The man called Jesus made mud and anointed my eyes and said to me, 'Go to Siloam and wash.' So I went and washed and received my sight." They said to him, "Where is he?" He said, "I do not know."

They brought to the Pharisees the man who had formerly been blind. Now it was a Sabbath day when Jesus made the mud and opened his eyes. So the Pharisees again asked him how he had received his sight. And he said to them, "He put mud on my eyes, and I washed, and I see." Some of the Pharisees said, "This man is not from God, for he does not keep the Sabbath." But others said, "How can a man who is a sinner do such signs?" And there was a division among them. So they said again to the blind man, "What do you say about him, since he has opened your eyes?" He said, "He is a prophet."

The Jews did not believe that he had been blind and had received his sight, until they called the parents of the man who had received his sight and asked them, "Is this your son, who you say was born blind? How then does he now see?" His parents answered, "We

know that this is our son and that he was born blind. But how he now sees we do not know, nor do we know who opened his eyes. Ask him; he is of age. He will speak for himself." (His parents said these things because they feared the Jews, for the Jews had already agreed that if anyone should confess Jesus to be Christ, he was to be put out of the synagogue.) Therefore his parents said, "He is of age; ask him."

So for the second time they called the man who had been blind and said to him, "Give glory to God. We know that this man is a sinner." He answered, "Whether he is a sinner I do not know. One thing I do know, that though I was blind, now I see." They said to him, "What did he do to you? How did he open your eyes?" He answered them, "I have told you already, and you would not listen. Why do you want to hear it again? Do you also want to become his disciples?" And they reviled him, saying, "You are his disciple, but we are disciples of Moses. We know that God has spoken to Moses, but as for this man, we do not know where he comes from." The man answered, "Why, this is an amazing thing! You do not know where he comes from, and yet he opened my eyes. We know that God does not listen to sinners, but if anyone is a worshiper of God and does his will, God listens to him. Never since the world began has it been heard that anyone opened the eyes of a man born blind. If this man were not from God, he could do nothing." They answered him, "You were born in utter sin, and would you teach us?" And they cast him out.

Jesus heard that they had cast him out, and having found him he said, "Do you believe in the Son of Man?" He answered, "And who is he, sir, that I may believe in him?" Jesus said to him, "You have seen him, and it is he who is speaking to you." He said, "Lord, I believe," and he worshiped him. Jesus said, "For judgment I came into this world, that those who do not see may see, and those who see may become blind." Some of the Pharisees near him heard these things, and said to him, "Are we also blind?" Jesus said to them, "If you were

blind, you would have no guilt; but now that you say, 'We see,' your guilt remains.

"Truly, truly, I say to you, he who does not enter the sheepfold by the door but climbs in by another way, that man is a thief and a robber. But he who enters by the door is the shepherd of the sheep. To him the gatekeeper opens. The sheep hear his voice, and he calls his own sheep by name and leads them out. When he has brought out all his own, he goes before them, and the sheep follow him, for they know his voice. A stranger they will not follow, but they will flee from him, for they do not know the voice of strangers." This figure of speech Jesus used with them, but they did not understand what he was saying to them.

So Jesus again said to them, "Truly, truly, I say to you, I am the door of the sheep. All who came before me are thieves and robbers, but the sheep did not listen to them. I am the door. If anyone enters by me, he will be saved and will go in and out and find pasture. The thief comes only to steal and kill and destroy. I came that they may have life and have it abundantly. I am the good shepherd. The good shepherd lays down his life for the sheep. He who is a hired hand and not a shepherd, who does not own the sheep, sees the wolf coming and leaves the sheep and flees, and the wolf snatches them and scatters them. He flees because he is a hired hand and cares nothing for the sheep. I am the good shepherd. I know my own and my own know me, just as the Father knows me and I know the Father; and I lay down my life for the sheep. And I have other sheep that are not of this fold. I must bring them also, and they will listen to my voice. So there will be one flock, one shepherd. For this reason the Father loves me, because I lay down my life that I may take it up again. No one takes it from me, but I lay it down of my own accord. I have authority to lay it down, and I have authority to take it up again. This charge I have received from my Father."

There was again a division among the Jews because of these

words. Many of them said, "He has a demon, and is insane; why listen to him?" Others said, "These are not the words of one who is oppressed by a demon. Can a demon open the eyes of the blind?"

At that time the Feast of Dedication took place at Jerusalem. It was winter, and Jesus was walking in the temple, in the colonnade of Solomon. So the Jews gathered around him and said to him, "How long will you keep us in suspense? If you are the Christ, tell us plainly." Jesus answered them, "I told you, and you do not believe. The works that I do in my Father's name bear witness about me, but you do not believe because you are not among my sheep. My sheep hear my voice, and I know them, and they follow me. I give them eternal life, and they will never perish, and no one will snatch them out of my hand. My Father, who has given them to me, is greater than all, and no one is able to snatch them out of the Father's hand. I and the Father, we are one."

The Jews picked up stones again to stone him. Jesus answered them, "I have shown you many good works from the Father; for which of them are you going to stone me?" The Jews answered him, "It is not for a good work that we are going to stone you but for blasphemy, because you, being a man, make yourself God." Jesus answered them, "Is it not written in your Law, 'I said, you are gods'? If he called them gods to whom the word of God came—and Scripture cannot be broken—do you say of him whom the Father consecrated and sent into the world, 'You are blaspheming,' because I said, 'I am the Son of God'? If I am not doing the works of my Father, then do not believe me; but if I do them, even though you do not believe me, believe the works, that you may know and understand that the Father is in me and I am in the Father." Again they sought to arrest him, but he escaped from their hands.

He went away again across the Jordan to the place where John had been baptizing at first, and there he remained. And many came to him. And they said, "John did no sign, but everything that John said about this man was true." And many believed in him there.

Session 9

Short Answer: John 9:1-10:42. Write the reference (chapter and verse) that best supports your answer (note: all questions and quotes are taken from the ESV translation).

1.0 Why was this particular man in John 9:1 born blind?

2.0 Assuming Jesus healed the blind man somewhere around the temple area, how far would the blind man have had to travel in order to wash (note: you may want to refer to the map, "Map 10: JERUSALEM" in the back of the ESV Study Bible)?

3.0 What were the different ways in which the once blind man referred to Jesus throughout John chapter 9?

4.1 Why did the once blind man's parents not want to get involved?

4.2 If the Jews would have done this thing his parents feared, what do you think they believed would have been the ramifications?

5.0 What did the once blind man do after Jesus had asked him if he believed in the Son of Man?

6.0 In John 10:1-21, Jesus identifies Himself as two different things. What are they and what does each do for the sheep (note: you may want to refer to the ESV Study Bible Notes)?

additional notes

Session 9

7.1 Why do the sheep follow, instead of flee, the Shepherd?

7.2 How has Jesus "plainly" told the Jews that He is the Christ?

7.3 Why didn't they believe (or hear) Him?

7.4 How do you think Jesus the Good Shepherd speaks to His sheep today?

8.1 Why did the Jews pick up stones to stone Jesus (John 10:31)?

8.2 What verse did Jesus make the claim that made the Jews want to stone Him?

9.1 Back during Jesus' time, how did the Jews refer to Scripture (hint: you may want to refer to the cross-references in John 10:34 and the ESV Study Bible Notes of those references)?

9.2 What were some various ways God spoke throughout the Bible (the answer to this question is not necessarily found in the immediate text)?

9.3 Today, how does God speak to His people Hint: Hebrews 1:1-2)?

9.4 When do you think Scripture became the sole Word of God?

10.0 To whom is Jesus most likely referring to as "gods" in John 10:34-35 (note: you may want to refer to the ESV Study Bible Notes and Cross-references)?

additional notes

Now a certain man was ill, Lazarus of Bethany, the village of Mary and her sister Martha. It was Mary who anointed the Lord with ointment and wiped his feet with her hair, whose brother Lazarus was ill. So the sisters sent to him, saying, "Lord, he whom you love is ill." But when Jesus heard it he said, "This illness does not lead to death. It is for the glory of God, so that the Son of God may be glorified through it."

Now Jesus loved Martha and her sister and Lazarus. So, when he heard that Lazarus was ill, he stayed two days longer in the place where he was. Then after this he said to the disciples, "Let us go to Judea again." The disciples said to him, "Rabbi, the Jews were just now seeking to stone you, and are you going there again?" Jesus answered, "Are there not twelve hours in the day? If anyone walks in the day, he does not stumble, because he sees the light of this world. But if anyone walks in the night, he stumbles, because the light is not in him." After saying these things, he said to them, "Our friend Lazarus has fallen asleep, but I go to awaken him." The disciples said to him, "Lord, if he has fallen asleep, he will recover." Now Jesus had spoken of his death, but they thought that he meant taking rest in sleep. Then Jesus told them plainly, "Lazarus has died, and for your sake I am glad that I was not there, so that you may believe. But let us go to him." So Thomas, called the Twin, said to his fellow disciples, "Let us also go, that we may die with him."

Now when Jesus came, he found that Lazarus had already been in the tomb four days. Bethany was near Jerusalem, about two miles off, and many of the Jews had come to Martha and Mary to console them concerning their brother. So when Martha heard that Jesus was coming, she went and met him, but Mary remained seated in the house. Martha said to Jesus, "Lord, if you had been here, my brother would not have died. But even now I know that whatever you ask from God, God will give you." Jesus said to her, "Your brother will rise again." Martha said to him, "I know that he will rise again in the resurrection on the last day." Jesus said to her, "I am the resurrection and the life. Whoever believes in me, though he die, yet shall he live,

and everyone who lives and believes in me shall never die. Do you believe this?" She said to him, "Yes, Lord; I believe that you are the Christ, the Son of God, who is coming into the world."

.   When she had said this, she went and called her sister Mary, saying in private, "The Teacher is here and is calling for you." And when she heard it, she rose quickly and went to him. Now Jesus had not yet come into the village, but was still in the place where Martha had met him. When the Jews who were with her in the house, consoling her, saw Mary rise quickly and go out, they followed her, supposing that she was going to the tomb to weep there. Now when Mary came to where Jesus was and saw him, she fell at his feet, saying to him, "Lord, if you had been here, my brother would not have died." When Jesus saw her weeping, and the Jews who had come with her also weeping, he was indignant in spirit and agitated.[9] And he said, "Where have you laid him?" They said to him, "Lord, come and see." Jesus wept. So the Jews said, "See how he loved him!" But some of them said, "Could not he who opened the eyes of the blind man also have kept this man from dying?"

Then Jesus, indignant again, came to the tomb. It was a cave, and a stone lay against it.[10] Jesus said, "Take away the stone." Martha, the sister of the dead man, said to him, "Lord, by this time there will be an odor, for he has been dead four days." Jesus said to her, "Did I not tell you that if you believed you would see the glory of God?" So they took away the stone. And Jesus lifted up his eyes and said, "Father, I thank you that you have heard me. I knew that you always hear me, but I said this on account of the people standing around, that they may believe that you sent me." When he had said these things, he cried out with a loud voice, "Lazarus, come out." The man who had died came out, his hands and feet bound with linen

---

[9] The ESV states, "When Jesus saw her weeping, and the Jews who had come with her also weeping, he was deeply moved in his spirit and greatly troubled."

[10] The ESV states, "Then Jesus, deeply moved again, came to the tomb. It was a cave, and a stone lay against it."

Session 10

John 11:1 – 12:50

strips, and his face wrapped with a cloth. Jesus said to them, "Unbind him, and let him go."

Many of the Jews therefore, who had come with Mary and had seen what he did, believed in him, but some of them went to the Pharisees and told them what Jesus had done. So the chief priests and the Pharisees gathered the council and said, "What are we to do? For this man performs many signs. If we let him go on like this, everyone will believe in him, and the Romans will come and take away both our place and our nation." But one of them, Caiaphas, who was high priest that year, said to them, "You know nothing at all. Nor do you understand that it is better for you that one man should die for the people, not that the whole nation should perish." He did not say this of his own accord, but being high priest that year he prophesied that Jesus would die for the nation, and not for the nation only, but also to gather into one the children of God who are scattered abroad. So from that day on they made plans to put him to death.

Jesus therefore no longer walked openly among the Jews, but went from there to the region near the wilderness, to a town called Ephraim, and there he stayed with the disciples.

Now the Passover of the Jews was at hand, and many went up from the country to Jerusalem before the Passover to purify themselves. They were looking for Jesus and saying to one another as they stood in the temple, "What do you think? That he will not come to the feast at all?" Now the chief priests and the Pharisees had given orders that if anyone knew where he was, he should let them know, so that they might arrest him.

Six days before the Passover, Jesus therefore came to Bethany, where Lazarus was, whom Jesus had raised from the dead. So they gave a dinner for him there. Martha served, and Lazarus was one of those reclining with him at table. Mary therefore took a pound of expensive ointment made from pure nard, and anointed the feet of Jesus and wiped his feet with her hair. The house was filled with the fragrance of the perfume. But Judas Iscariot, one of his disciples (he

88

who was about to betray him), said, "Why was this ointment not sold for three hundred denarii and given to the poor?" He said this, not because he cared about the poor, but because he was a thief, and having charge of the moneybag he used to help himself to what was put into it. Jesus said, "Leave her alone, so that she may keep it for the day of my burial. For the poor you always have with you, but you do not always have me."

When the large crowd of the Jews learned that Jesus was there, they came, not only on account of him but also to see Lazarus, whom he had raised from the dead. So the chief priests made plans to put Lazarus to death as well, because on account of him many of the Jews were going away and believing in Jesus.

The next day the large crowd that had come to the feast heard that Jesus was coming to Jerusalem. So they took branches of palm trees and went out to meet him, crying out, "Hosanna! Blessed is he who comes in the name of the Lord, even the King of Israel!" And Jesus found a young donkey and sat on it, just as it is written, "Fear not, daughter of Zion; behold, your king is coming, sitting on a donkey's colt!"

His disciples did not understand these things at first, but when Jesus was glorified, then they remembered that these things had been written about him and had been done to him. The crowd that had been with him when he called Lazarus out of the tomb and raised him from the dead continued to bear witness. The reason why the crowd went to meet him was that they heard he had done this sign. So the Pharisees said to one another, "You see that you are gaining nothing. Look, the world has gone after him."

Now among those who went up to worship at the feast were some Greeks. So these came to Philip, who was from Bethsaida in Galilee, and asked him, "Sir, we wish to see Jesus." Philip went and told Andrew; Andrew and Philip went and told Jesus. And Jesus answered them, "The hour has come for the Son of Man to be glorified. Truly, truly, I say to you, unless a grain of wheat falls into the earth and dies, it remains alone; but if it dies, it bears much fruit.

Session 10

John 11:1 – 12:50

Whoever loves his life loses it, and whoever hates his life in this world will keep it for eternal life. If anyone serves me, he must follow me; and where I am, there will my servant be also. If anyone serves me, the Father will honor him.

"Now is my soul troubled. And what shall I say? 'Father, save me from this hour'? But for this purpose I have come to this hour. Father, glorify your name." Then a voice came from heaven: "I have glorified it, and I will glorify it again." The crowd that stood there and heard it said that it had thundered. Others said, "An angel has spoken to him." Jesus answered, "This voice has come for your sake, not mine. Now is the judgment of this world; now will the ruler of this world be cast out. And I, when I am lifted up from the earth, will draw all people to myself." He said this to show by what kind of death he was going to die. So the crowd answered him, "We have heard from the Law that the Christ remains forever. How can you say that the Son of Man must be lifted up? Who is this Son of Man?" So Jesus said to them, "The light is among you for a little while longer. Walk while you have the light, lest darkness overtake you. The one who walks in the darkness does not know where he is going. While you have the light, believe in the light, that you may become sons of light."

When Jesus had said these things, he departed and hid himself from them. Though he had done so many signs before them, they still did not believe in him, so that the word spoken by the prophet Isaiah might be fulfilled: "Lord, who has believed what he heard from us, and to whom has the arm of the Lord been revealed?"

Therefore they could not believe. For again Isaiah said, "He has blinded their eyes and hardened their heart, lest they see with their eyes, and understand with their heart, and turn, and I would heal them."

Isaiah said these things because he saw his glory and spoke of him. Nevertheless, many even of the authorities believed in him, but for fear of the Pharisees they did not confess it, so that they would not be put out of the synagogue; for they loved the glory that comes from man more than the glory that comes from God.

90

And Jesus cried out and said, "Whoever believes in me, believes not in me but in him who sent me. And whoever sees me sees him who sent me. I have come into the world as light, so that whoever believes in me may not remain in darkness. If anyone hears my words and does not keep them, I do not judge him; for I did not come to judge the world but to save the world. The one who rejects me and does not receive my words has a judge; the word that I have spoken will judge him on the last day. For I have not spoken on my own authority, but the Father who sent me has himself given me a commandment—what to say and what to speak. And I know that his commandment is eternal life. What I say, therefore, I say as the Father has told me."

The following quotes are taken from some of the most prominent and respected grammatical commentaries:

"The rendering of the main clause, "Jesus ... became angry in spirit and very agitated" requires discussion, not to say justification, in view of its departure from most English translations. There has been an unusual disagreement between the English and German traditions of understanding this passage."[11]

"It is impossible to conclude that anything less than anger is meant here [v. 33] or in verse 38. The use of this verb and its cognates, both in the New Testament and elsewhere, clearly implies anger. Evidently the translations which attempt to remove the concept of anger from these verses do so on theological [biases] rather than linguistic or exegetical grounds. The actual basis for Jesus' anger is not explicitly indicated, but the contents of verse 33 and verse 37 imply that it was caused by the immature faith of the Jews who were present."[12]

---

[11] Beasley-Murray, G. R. (2002). *Vol. 36: Word Biblical Commentary : John*. Word Biblical Commentary (192). Dallas: Word, Incorporated.
[12] Newman, B. M., & Nida, E. A. (1993). *A handbook on the Gospel of John*. Helps for translators; UBS handbook series (371). New York: United Bible Societies.

"What does the crucial word *embrimaomai* actually mean? In extra-biblical Greek, it can refer to the *snorting* of horses; as applied to human beings, it invariably suggests anger, outrage or emotional indignation. In the New Testament, it occurs twice in this chapter (*cf.* v. 38), and elsewhere only in Matthew 9:30; Mark 1:43; 14:5; and in a textual variant to Matthew 12:18. Not only this word but its cognates as well move in this sphere of meaning. Beasley-Murray (pp. 192–193) points out that German translations get it right; most English translations soften the passage to 'he groaned in spirit', 'he sighed heavily', 'he was deeply touched' or, as here, 'he was deeply moved in spirit'—all without linguistic justification. It is lexically inexcusable to reduce this emotional upset to the effects of empathy, grief, pain or the like."[13]

"But the reaction of Jesus to that kind of wailing by the mourners was hardly empathetic support. The result was that Jesus became "disgusted" or "angered" (the Greek is *embrimasthai*) in his spirit and "perturbed" *(tarassein)* by the actions of the people (11:33)."[14]

"On the way to the tomb, Jesus **wept,** breaking out into tears. This was silent weeping in contrast to Christ's audible weeping over Jerusalem (Lk 19:41). The Jews who were present saw in the weeping a proof of Jesus' great affection for Lazarus, but they saw in it also evidence of his limitation. He had given sight to the blind (Jn 11:9), but death was too great for his powers (v. 37). Perhaps in the second **groaning** there was a mingling of indignation at this shortsighted view of his power."[15]

---

[13] Carson, D. A. (1991). *The Gospel according to John* (415). Leicester, England; Grand Rapids, Mich.: Inter-Varsity Press; W.B. Eerdmans.

[14] Borchert, G. L. (2001). *Vol. 25A: John 1-11* (electronic ed.). Logos Library System; The New American Commentary (359). Nashville: Broadman & Holman Publishers.

[15] Pfeiffer, C. F., & Harrison, E. F. (1962). *The Wycliffe Bible commentary : New Testament* (Jn 11:33). Chicago: Moody Press.

According to the original language, it is clear that Jesus was very indignant and agitated. The question is not what emotion Jesus felt that caused His weeping; but rather, what caused Him to feel this intense anger? Jesus' disgust produced tears that welled up in His eyes that streamed down His cheeks. It is only in the context of John chapter eleven that the student of the Bible can unlock the mystery concerning the origin of His frustrated tears. The sacrificial Lamb's incarnate ministry was nearing its end upon the cross which understandably would have had Jesus' emotional sensitivity at an all-time high. He was about to experience the full wrath of God by taking on the sin of the world; and maybe the greatest dread of all, be separated from His beloved Father in broken fellowship. Lazarus' death, burial, and resurrection was to benefit Jesus' followers. Lazarus' death was to glorify the Son of God in order to glorify God by revealing the Father. Did those that had known Jesus for over three years still not really know or believe in His name? In just a little over a week would they think, just as they had with Lazarus, that the sting of death had defeated the Resurrection and the Life? Jesus had so little time to teach those who had so little faith. Instead of pouring out His anger on the ignorant beloved, He expressed self-controlled compassion by pouring out tears of anger upon His cheeks. The climax of Jesus' earthly ministry would be perceived as the ultimate defeat through death upon a cross; but in actually, it would give Life through a victorious Resurrection. Jesus Christ is the Resurrection and the Life!

Session 10

1.0   What spiritual realities might Jesus have revealed by raising Lazarus from the dead (hint: you may want to refer to the brief summary notes found in the ESV Study Bible Notes at the beginning of this new section. You may notice that the summary notes at the beginning of each section correspond to the outline for each book of the Bible located in the introduction section of each book, and are shaded within the notes)?

2.1   What did Jesus explain the purpose of Lazarus' illness was when He said to His disciples, "This illness does not lead to death?"

2.2   How do you think Jesus has ultimately been glorified and brought God glory (note: this answer is not necessarily found within the immediate text)?

3.0   List at least two reasons why you think the disciples may not have wanted to travel back to Judea?

4.0   Why do you think "fallen asleep" is an appropriate way to describe Lazarus' death?

5.1   How many days did Jesus stay where He was after He heard Lazarus was sick?

5.2   How do you explain that Lazarus was dead for four days (John 11:17)?

additional notes

Short Answer: John 11-12:50. Write the reference (chapter and verse) that best supports your answer (note: all questions and quotes are taken from the ESV translation).

6.1 When Jesus was speaking with Martha the first time, what did Jesus say would happen to the person who "believes in me"?

6.2 How does Jesus' claim in John 11:25-26 differ from what Jesus was saying in John 5:21, 24?

7.1 What was the deep emotion that Jesus had when he saw Mary and the Jews weeping and when He can to Lazarus' tomb (note: you may want to refer to the above quotes and provided translation in your workbook as well as the ESV Study Bible Notes, footnotes, and cross-references, and provided article for v. 33, 38 to help answer this question)?

7.2 How did Jesus outwardly express this emotion?

7.3 How did the Jews misinterpret Jesus' tears?

7.4 Why do you think Jesus felt the way that He did?

8.1 What two ways did the Jews respond to Jesus raising Lazarus from the dead?

8.2 What two ways do you think people often respond today to Jesus' being raised from the dead?

9.0 What concerns did the Pharisees have in letting Jesus continue to perform miraculous signs, potentially leading to "everyone will believe in Him" (note: you may want to refer to the ESV Study Bible Notes)?

additional notes

Session 10

10.1 What did Caiaphas believe he was saying in John 11:50?

10.2 Explain the truth of his prophecy.

11.0 Approximately how much (in today's currency) was the perfume worth that was poured on Jesus' feet?

12.1 Why do you think the crowd took palm branches to go out to meet Jesus (note: you may want to refer to the ESV Study Bible Notes)?

12.2 What does the word "Hosanna" mean (note: you may want to refer to the text notes and ESV Study Bible Notes)?

13.1 What do you think Jesus meant in John 12:24-26?

13.2 What kind of man will keep his life for eternal life?

14.1 Where else does John reference that "the Son of Man must be lifted up"?

14.2 What do you think Jesus means by the statement, "The Son of Man must be lifted up" (note: you may want to refer to the ESV cross-references and the ESV Study Bible Notes)?

additional notes

Preface to Sessions 11a through 11d

The next five chapters (John 13 – 17) contain the last initiative action and teaching of Jesus' earthly ministry. These five chapters contain Jesus instituting the first of His two ordinances of the church in an upper room, followed by the detailed teaching relating to the ordinance. His earthly ministry culminated with an intimate prayer to His Father (John 17). The upper room ordinance was the climactic summary of His earthly ministry. This workbook treats the last few hours of Jesus' incarnate ministry as one session broken into four sections (i.e. Session 11a, 11b, 11c, and 11d). The student will notice that the numbers of the questions are progressive through all four sessions.

The first twelve chapters of John record the first three plus years of Jesus' earthly ministry while the last half of the book of John records His final week. This John discipleship tool has divided Session 11 into four interrelated sub-sessions in order to try and keep the conversation Christ had with the Disciples within the context of the ordinance He just instituted for the church in the upper room (i.e. 11a, 11b, 11c, and 11d). As the student of the Bible works through Sessions 11a – 11d, it will be necessary to not only consider a particular passage within the context of the current session, but also within the other related sessions. It may prove beneficial to try and read John 13:1 through John 17:26 in one sitting several times while working through Sessions 11a – 11d.

John 13:1-30

Now before the Feast of the Passover, when Jesus knew that his hour had come to depart out of this world to the Father, he now showed them the full extent of his love.[16] During supper, when the devil had already put it into the heart of Judas Iscariot, Simon's son, to betray him, Jesus, knowing that the Father had given all things into his hands, and that he had come from God and was going back to God, rose from supper. He laid aside his outer garments, and taking a towel, tied it around his waist. Then he poured water into a basin and began to wash the disciples' feet and to wipe them with the towel that was wrapped around him. He came to Simon Peter, who said to him, "Lord, do you wash my feet?" Jesus answered him, "What I am doing you do not understand now, but afterward you will understand." Peter said to him, "You shall never wash my feet." Jesus answered him, "If I do not wash you, you have no share with me." Simon Peter said to him, "Lord, not my feet only but also my hands and my head!" Jesus said to him, "The one who has bathed only needs to wash his feet because he is completely clean.[17] And you are clean, but not every one of you." For he knew who was to betray him; that was why he said, "Not all of you are clean."

When he had washed their feet and put on his outer garments and resumed his place, he said to them, "Do you understand what I have done to you? You call me Teacher and Lord, and you are right, for so I am. If I then, your Lord and Teacher, have washed your feet, you also ought to wash one another's feet. For I have given you an example, that you also should do just as I have done to you. Truly, truly, I say to you, a servant is not greater than his master, nor is a messenger greater than the one who sent him. Now that you realize

---

[16] The ESV states, "Now before the Feast of the Passover, when Jesus knew that his hour had come to depart out of this world to the Father, having loved his own who were in the world, he loved them to the end."

[17] The ESV states, "The one who has bathed does not need to wash, except for his feet, but is completely clean."

John 13:1-30

that what I have said is true, blessed are you if you put them into practice.[18] I am not speaking of all of you I know whom I have chosen. But the Scripture will be fulfilled, 'He who ate my bread has lifted his heel against me.' I am telling you this now, before it takes place, that when it does take place you may believe that I am. Truly, truly, I say to you, whoever receives the one I send receives me, and whoever receives me receives the one who sent me."

After saying these things, Jesus was troubled in his spirit, and testified, "Truly, truly, I say to you, one of you will betray me." The disciples looked at one another, uncertain of whom he spoke. One of his disciples, whom Jesus loved, was reclining at table at Jesus' side, so Simon Peter motioned to him to ask Jesus of whom he was speaking. So that disciple, leaning back against Jesus, said to him, "Lord, who is it?" Jesus answered, "It is he to whom I will give this morsel of bread when I have dipped it." So when he had dipped the morsel, he gave it to Judas, the son of Simon Iscariot. Then after he had taken the morsel, Satan entered into him. Jesus said to him, "What you are going to do, do quickly." Now no one at the table knew why he said this to him. Some thought that, because Judas had the moneybag, Jesus was telling him, "Buy what we need for the feast," or that he should give something to the poor. So, after receiving the morsel of bread, he immediately went out. And it was night.

---

[18] The ESV states, "If you know these things, blessed are you if you do them."

additional notes

Session 11a

> **Short Answer: John 13:1 – 30.** Write the reference (chapter and verse) that best supports your answer (note: all questions and quotes are taken from the ESV translation).

1.1 According to John 11:55, why did many people go up to Jerusalem before the Passover?

The Greek words *niptō* and *louō* in John 13:1-17: The word that means "to wash" is *niptō*. Partial washing is at issue here. Running or flowing water, especially from springs, is preferred for washing. Ritual purity in the approach to Deity imposes the need for cultic washing. This is important in the OT (cf. Ex. 30:18-19; Dt. 21:6). Judaism extends the OT rules, e.g., by requiring washing of the hands before meals. In the NT *niptō* means partial washing. In the foot-washing *niptō* is partial washing as distinct from *louō* (i.e having a complete cleansing bath, Jn 13:5-11). By His action here Jesus sets an example of menial service. But the action also has symbolical significance. Christ's death gives full cleansing (*louō*), so that there is no need for partial cleansing (*niptō*).[19]

2.1 What is the Greek word translated "wash" in John 13:1-17?

2.2 What is the Greek word translated "bath" in John 13:1-17?

2.3 After reading the above article, what is the difference between these two Greek words *niptō* and *louō*?

---

[19] Modified excerpts from The Theological Dictionary of the New Testament, abridged in one volume, page 635.

3.1 According to John 13:1, when it was before the Feast of the Passover and Jesus knew that his hour had come to depart to the Father, what was the action of footwashing to show (note: you may want to refer to the provided translation in your workbook)?

3.2 According to your understanding of the Gospel message, what do you think Jesus has done to "show the full extent of His love" (the answer to this question is not necessarily directly found within our immediate text)?

additional notes

Session 11a

John 3:8-9: Jesus' Conversation with Peter

Recorded within the book of John, Jesus Christ claimed and demonstrated to have a special union and fellowship with God the Father. Jesus explained that the only way in which others could have a union and fellowship with God was through Him... alone... period. He is the only way to God. Please look up and read the following verses (if you have not read them already) that demonstrate that there is no way to God except through Jesus Christ:

Before the 1ˢᵗ Passover feast in Jesus' public ministry: John 1:4-5; 1:12-13; 1:14; 1:18; 1:37-39.

The 1ˢᵗ full year of Jesus' public ministry: John 3:13; 3:16-21; 3:31-36; 4:10; and 4:34.

The 2ⁿᵈ full year of Jesus' public ministry: John 5:17; 5:19-23; 5:24-27; 5:30; 5:36b-38; 5:43a; and 5:45-47.

Final year of Jesus' public ministry: John 6:27 with 6:29; 6:32; 6:35-40; 6:44-51; 6:53-58; 6:62; 6:66-69; 7:16-18; 7:28-29; 7:33-34; 8:12; 8:13-18; 8:19; 8:21; 8:23-24; 8:25-26; 8:27-29; 8:38; 8:39-40; 8:42-47; 8:49-51; 8:54-56; 9:3-5; 10:25-30; 10:32; 10:36-38; 11:25-26; and 11:41.

Final week of Jesus' public ministry before the washing of the disciples feet: John 12:23-26; 12:27-28; 12:35-36a; 12:44-46; 12:47-50.

As observed from above, Jesus steadily and increasingly taught that He was the only way to God the Father as He approached His final hours of His earthly ministry. Peter, who had a strong desire to serve God and enter His Kingdom, understood that Jesus was the only way to enter the Kingdom of God. It was Peter's desire to enter into God's kingdom, along with his understanding that Jesus is the only way to God the Father, that transformed Peter's heart when Jesus said, "Unless I wash you, you have *no part with me*" (emphasis mine). In John 13:8, the Greek word translated "part" or "share" (i.e. *meros*)

relates to the eschatological salvation of one's soul. The Greek word "μέρος [meros] is used among Jews in reference to having a part in an inheritance, notably in the promise land, and then eschatologically in the kingdom of God." Peter understood Jesus saying that the only way to God was to "have a place with someone,"[20] namely Christ. In essence, what Peter heard Christ telling him was if Jesus did not wash his feet, he would never enter the Kingdom of God (i.e. in the Christian vernacular, 'he would never go to heaven'). He would never be able to be with, know, or serve God in the Kingdom. The Jews were looking for their Messiah because they were yearning to enter the Kingdom of God. Peter truly believed Jesus was the Messiah and was his only hope to enter the Kingdom of God. For instance, when questioned by Jesus, "'But what about you?' he asked. 'Who do you say I am?' Peter answered, 'The Messiah of God'" (Luke 9:20 with Matthew 16:15 and Mark 8:29). Also, on one occasion when Christ questioned His disciples and asked if they would like to leave Him, "Simon Peter answered him, 'Lord, to whom shall we go? You have the words of eternal life. We believe and know that you are the Holy One of God'" (John 6:68-69). "What could footwashing possibly symbolize as to be so serious that it would prevent Peter from sharing in the inheritance of the Messiah and therefore disqualify his entrance into God's Kingdom?"[21] Footwashing is a physical action symbolic of Jesus' humble obedience of sacrifice on the cross. Disciples of Christ are made "clean" (13:10) by their acceptance of Jesus and his substitutionary death through faith.

4.0 **After reading the above article, why do you think Peter quickly changed his emphatic position in John 13:9** (hint: you may want to consider the meaning of Jesus' statement in John 13:8b)**?**

(continue to read the following and then answer questions 5 - 11)

---

[20] Word Biblical Commentary on John by George R. Beasley-Murray, pages 233-234
[21] A Greek-English Lexicon of the New Testament and Other Early Christian Literature, by Walter Bauer, page 506

The Meaning of Footwashing

The ESV Study Notes are a type of commentary. Commentaries, Bible Dictionaries, and Bible Encyclopedias can play an important role in helping the interpreter of the Bible better understand the truth of Scripture. However, there is a word of caution that should be issued on the use of Commentaries. As described in the preface of this workbook, there are many different ways to approach the Bible in order to interpret the meaning. Unless the student of the Bible knows the hermeneutic of the commentator, great care should be given concerning their interpretation expressed in their commentary. Comparing the commentator's interpretation in light of the truth of the Scriptures will reveal their prescribed hermeneutic. This will expose whether the commentator's hermeneutic is Biblically sound and consistent. Though many scholars can offer great historical, contextual, and grammatical insight on various passages, this does not mean that their interpretation is always accurate. The student of the Bible should develop and then use their own sound biblical hermeneutic to compare whether the commentator has properly interpreted the truth of the Scriptures.

In interpreting the meaning of footwashing, Bible scholars often fall into one of two camps. Many scholars have understood footwashing to be a humble action of Jesus Christ in which He intended to teach the Disciples that they should be humble (John 13:12-17). Other biblical scholars have understood footwashing to be a lasting symbolic physical action for the church instituted by Jesus Christ in the upper room during His last supper. For when Jesus instituted the footwashing, He also instituted the Bread, and the Cup, and the Agape Feast (John 13:6-11). These two views, the humility teaching (vv. 12-17) and the ordinance teaching (vv. 6-11), should not be viewed as an either/or proposition. Both teachings are valid and complimentary to the other. When these two views are interpreted together, they can help the Bible student understand the spiritual truth of footwashing. Footwashing is the first action of the upper room ordinance and is related to Christ's ultimate act of humility.

Most proponents of the humility teaching emphasize vv. 12-17 along with the cultural Semitic attitude toward washing feet. The following quotes communicate this particular position:

"In the ancient Near East, where roads were dusty and sandals were the common footwear, making provision for guests or travelers to wash their feet was an act of common hospitality (Gen. 18:4; 19:2; 24:32; Luke 7:36–50; cf. John 12:1–8). The washing of feet also became part of the purification rituals required of priests prior to entering the sanctuary or approaching the altar (Exod. 30:19–21; 40:31). Jesus performed the menial task of washing his disciples' feet while they were at table during the Last Supper. He commended his action as an example of the type of service the disciples should provide to each other (John 13:1–20)." [22]

"FOOTWASHING: An act necessary for comfort and cleanliness for any who have traveled dusty Palestinian roads wearing sandals. Customarily, a host provided guests with water for washing their own feet (Judg. 19:21; Luke 7:44, where the complaint was that Simon had not provided water). Footwashing was regarded as so lowly a task that it could not be required of a Hebrew slave. In this context the statement of John the Baptist that he was unworthy to untie the sandal (to wash the feet) of the One coming after him (Mark 1:7) indicates great humility." [23]

"In ancient times, all the roads were either dusty or muddy, so it was a common courtesy to provide footwashing for visitors. In Christian circles, washing someone's feet came to symbolize humility (John 13:15). Be prepared: Service that pleases Christ is often done at personal inconvenience and not for personal profit." [24]

---

[22] Tucker, J. T. (2000). Footwashing. In D. N. Freedman (Ed.), Eerdmans dictionary of the Bible (D. N. Freedman, Ed.) (468). Grand Rapids, MI: W.B. Eerdmans.

[23] Brand, C., Draper, C., England, A., Bond, S., Clendenen, E. R., Butler, T. C., & Latta, B. (2003). Holman Illustrated Bible Dictionary (592). Nashville, TN: Holman Bible Publishers.

[24] MacArthur, J. F., Jr. (1997, c1994.). Different by Design (95–96). Wheaton, IL: Victor Books.

"John was writing his gospel for Greeks and so he explains that these jars were there to provide water for the purifying ceremonies of the Jews. Strict Jews washed the hands before a meal and between each course. First water was poured in such a way that it ran from the wrist to the finger-tips. This was done with each hand in turn; and then each palm was cleansed by rubbing it with the fist of the other hand. The Jewish ceremonial law insisted that this should be done not only at the beginning of a meal but also between courses. If it was not done the hands were technically unclean." [25]

"The example Jesus gives the disciples in washing their feet (13:12–20) is the pattern of sacrificial and costly service. The key word for this service is agape [i.e. the Greek word for love], given in the command that disciples should "love one another" (13:34–35) and thereby witness to the world." [26]

"Water was also used for washing and bathing, serving the needs of hygiene, refreshment, and ritual purification. Jews of Jesus' time washed their hands before meals in accordance with religious prescription (Mark 7:3), and guests were offered water for footwashing (Luke 7:44)—a service commonly performed by a servant (cf. John 13:5). OT laws prescribe ablutions for various types of contaminating conditions, including various skin diseases (Lev. 14:8), bodily emissions (Lev. 15:1-21), and contact with dead or 'unclean' animals (11:1-39). Pilate declared his innocence through a symbolic act of handwashing (Matt. 27:24)." [27]

"Christ certainly humbled Himself through obedience to the Father – even to the point of death on a cross (Philippians 2:1-11). So while it is true that footwashing was a menial humiliating task not even fit for

---

[25] The Gospel of John : Volume 1. 2000 (W. Barclay, lecturer in the University of Glasgow, Ed.). The Daily study Bible series, Rev. ed. (98–99). Philadelphia: The Westminster Press.

[26] Green, J. B., McKnight, S., & Marshall, I. H. (1992). Dictionary of Jesus and the Gospels (750). Downers Grove, Ill.: InterVarsity Press.

[27] Achtemeier, P. J., Harper & Row, P., & Society of Biblical Literature. (1985). Harper's Bible dictionary (1st ed.) (1121). San Francisco: Harper & Row.

the lowliest of Hebrew slaves, it seems likely that the footwashing was more than just an object lesson on humility (cf. vv. 6–11)." [28]

There are several aspects of the footwashing passage that indicate this action is more than a common ancient custom Jesus simply used in order to teach a lesson on humility:

- John 13:1 states that the footwashing pictures Jesus' full extent of his love. Does giving an object lesson on humility show Jesus' full extent of His love? No, footwashing is tied to Jesus' action that shows the full extent of His love: the cross, burial, resurrection, and exaltation.

- The timing of footwashing: Footwashing was the beginning of Jesus' final action and teaching before the cross. Jesus instituted the bread and cup at the very same time and place He instituted the footwashing. Also, it was not customary to get up from dinner and begin washing feet. The Disciples would have already washed their feet upon entering the upper room.

- When Jesus was just about to wash Peter's feet He said, "What I am doing you do not understand now, but afterward you will understand." Could the Disciples not understand a cultural custom? Could the Disciples not understand a teaching on humility? Of course they could! But they would not fully understand the symbolic meaning of Jesus' action until after He went to the cross, was resurrected, ascended to heaven, and receiving the Holy Spirit.

- There are consequences and blessings associated with footwashing. "If I do not wash you, you have no share with me" and "If you know these things, blessed are you if you do them" (John 13:8-17). And furthermore, the consequence and blessing only apply to believers (John 13:10, 18).

---

[28] Utley, R. J. D. (1999). Vol. Volume 4: The Beloved Disciple's Memoirs and Letters: The Gospel of John, I, II, and III John. Study Guide Commentary Series (119). Marshall, Texas: Bible Lessons International.

111

- If footwashing was an object lesson on humility, why did the Disciples start disputing which of them was to be regarded as the greatest immediately after Jesus washed their feet (Luke 22:24-27)? And furthermore, Jesus gave them no rebuke. This would have been a perfect time to reiterate the supposed object lesson on humility; but instead, He teaches them about their role in the future Kingdom of God.

These are a few observations of the footwashing passage that indicate this may be more than just a mere object lesson on humility. The following quotes represent a possible deeper meaning behind footwashing than simply an object lesson on humility:

"Peter and the others will understand later—or, better, 'after these things' (Gk. meta tauta). This [i.e. these things] does not refer to the footwashing, but to the passion to which the footwashing points. After Jesus' death/exaltation, and certainly after the descent of the Spirit who comes in consequence of that tragic and glorious event, they will understand."[29]

"When Jesus finished washing the disciples' feet, he made it clear that the act was to be perpetuated. The term used in 13:14 to indicate that the disciples ought to wash one another's feet is ὀφείλετε, which expresses not an option but an obligation. The Lord's actual command (v 14b) uses the word 'ought' (ὀφείλω), a word used to express moral obligation (cf. 1 John 4:11; Eph 5:28; Matt 18:28). An accurate translation would be 'owe' or 'indebted.' 'You are also indebted to wash one another's feet.' The present tense of ὀφείλετε and νίπτειν points to the need to continue or perpetuate the act of washing feet."[30]

"As with the crucifixion, so with the footwashing: each is simultaneously an act of God by which human beings are freed or

[29] Carson, D. A. (1991). The Gospel according to John (454–476). Leicester, England; Grand Rapids, Mich.: Inter-Varsity Press; W.B. Eerdmans.
[30] Grace Seminary. (1985; 2002). Vol. 6: Grace Theological Journal Volume 6 (419–420). Grace Seminary.

cleansed—whether in reality (the cross) or in symbol (the footwashing)—and an example that Jesus' followers are to emulate."[31]

"Since Peter certainly understood the humility involved in Jesus' action, we may assume that more than humility was in view. The emphasis in v. 16 is not upon the serving of the slave, but upon the position of the master. It again stresses his authority to do just as he did. Humility is involved, but the picture intended by Jesus involves cleansing more than humility, the latter of which is the proper mindset for the former."[32]

"Jesus himself washed the feet of his disciples at the Last Supper, symbolizing not only the humble service that would be required of them but also the cleansing of human sin which his death would affect (John 13:3–17)."[33]

In modern culture, it may be difficult to understand how someone could be considered completely clean even though their feet may need to be washed (John 13:10). Imagine someone in our culture taking a bath, getting dressed, walking outside, and stepping in some mud. It would not be necessary to take a bath in order to enter their house. Someone who has had a bath would simply have to take off their muddy shoes. They are completely clean. Having muddy shoes does not make the person unclean; and having dirty feet during Jesus' day did not make someone unclean either. Jesus stated in John 13:10 that a person who has had a bath is completely clean. Therefore they would only have to wash his feet upon entering a house. He did not say that they are mostly clean; He said they are **completely** clean.

---

[31] Carson, D. A. (1991). The Gospel according to John (454–476). Leicester, England; Grand Rapids, Mich.: Inter-Varsity Press; W.B. Eerdmans.

[32] Grace Seminary. (1985; 2002). Vol. 6: Grace Theological Journal Volume 6 (431). Grace Seminary.

[33] Myers, A. C. (1987). The Eerdmans Bible dictionary (390). Grand Rapids, Mich.: Eerdmans.

In the footwashing passage, cleanliness is referencing spiritual cleanliness of the heart (i.e. inward spiritual righteousness, not external carnal cleanliness). This can be seen by Jesus' comment in verse 11. The bath that provides spiritual cleanliness is the bath given by Jesus Christ through faith. This is the only spiritual bath that can completely and permanently cleanse. And when Jesus has given you a spiritual bath, you are completely cleansed of past, present, and future sins! One bath provides a complete spiritual cleansing forever. Footwashing symbolically pictures that one has been spiritually bathed by Jesus Christ and therefore has an eschatological connection to Jesus. A partial cleansing certainly does not symbolically picture this kind of relationship to Jesus. Footwashing does not cleanse, but only symbolically pictures that one has been completely spiritually cleansed through faith in Jesus.

Jesus humbled himself to provide a complete spiritual bath in order to bring us to God (Philippians 2:3-11 and 1 Peter 3:18). Footwashing pictures how Christ "humbled himself by becoming obedient to the point of death, even death on a cross" (Philippians 2:8). Jesus said, "And for their sake I sanctify myself, that they also may be sanctified in truth" (John 17:19). Through Jesus' humble obedient action, believers have been completely spiritually cleansed through faith in Christ! Jesus has provided a physical action that His followers are to repeatedly perform in order to picture this spiritual reality; namely, they have been spiritually cleansed through faith in Christ due to His humble obedient act of the cross.

additional notes

Session 11a

Short Answer: John 13:1 – 30. Write the reference (chapter and verse) that best supports your answer (note: all questions and quotes are taken from the ESV translation).

5.1 **What condition (clean or unclean) is the individual who only needs to wash his feet** (hint: you may want to read the provided translation to help answer this question)**?**

5.2 **What do you think the Jews understood it meant to be "clean"?**

5.3 **Did Jesus declare the Disciples to be completely clean before or after He washed their feet?**

5.4 **What does footwashing symbolically demonstrate?**

6.1 **Spiritually speaking, what is the "dirt" which determines whether an individual is spiritually clean or unclean** (Since the John 13 passage is referencing spiritual cleanliness and does not reference what caused our original uncleanly state, the answer to this question is not directly found or stated within the immediate text)**?**

6.2 **How is an individual spiritually cleansed of this spiritual dirt in order to become spiritually clean/bathed** (The answer to this question is not necessarily directly found within our immediate text. You may want to refer to John 15:3 with Ephesians 5:26 and Ephesians 2:8-9 with Romans 10:17 along with the ESV Study Bible Notes)**?**

7.1 **What was Jesus saying in John 13:14-15?**

7.2 **What had Jesus just done to His disciples?**

7.3 **What did Jesus say would happen to people if they put this truth into practice (John 13:17)?**

additional notes

Session 11a

Short Answer: John 13:1 – 30. Write the reference (chapter and verse) that best supports your answer (note: all questions and quotes are taken from the ESV translation).

8.1   What did not apply to Judas when Jesus said, "I am not speaking of all of you" in John 13:18 (hint: consider what Jesus just said in John 13:17 and review question 7.3 of this Session)?

8.2   Why did some of the disciples think Jesus told Judas, "What you are going to do, do quickly"?

9.1   Who does an individual "receive" when they receive anyone sent by Jesus?

9.2   "Whoever receives" Jesus also "receives" who else?

10.1   What other two physical symbols that represent spiritual realities did Jesus institute in the very same place at the very same time that He instituted the footwashing (hint: you may want to cross-reference the synoptics on the account of Jesus dipping his morsel of bread and giving it to Judas)?

10.2   What do these other two physical symbols spiritually represent?

10.3   Why do you think most churches continue to observe these later two symbols but do not observe footwashing?

11.0   What did Judas do immediately after he received the morsel of bread from Jesus?

additional notes

When he had gone out, Jesus said, "Now is the Son of Man glorified, and God is glorified in him. If God is glorified in him, God will also glorify him in himself, and glorify him at once. Little children, yet a little while I am with you. You will seek me, and just as I said to the Jews, so now I also say to you, 'Where I am going you cannot come.' A new commandment I give to you, that you love one another: just as I have loved you, you also are to love one another. By this all people will know that you are my disciples, if you have love for one another.

"Simon Peter said to him, "Lord, where are you going?" Jesus answered him, "Where I am going you cannot follow me now, but you will follow afterward." Peter said to him, "Lord, why can I not follow you now? I will lay down my life for you." Jesus answered, "Will you lay down your life for me? Truly, truly, I say to you, the rooster will not crow till you have denied me three times.

"Let not your hearts be troubled. Believe in God; believe also in me. In my Father's house are many rooms. If it were not so, would I have told you that I go to prepare a place for you? And if I go and prepare a place for you, I will come again and will take you to myself, that where I am you may be also. And you know the way to where I am going." Thomas said to him, "Lord, we do not know where you are going. How can we know the way?" Jesus said to him, "I am the way, and the truth, and the life. No one comes to the Father except through me. If you had known me, you would have known my Father also. From now on you do know him and have seen him."

Philip said to him, "Lord, show us the Father, and it is enough for us." Jesus said to him, "Have I been with you so long, and you still do not know me, Philip? Whoever has seen me has seen the Father. How can you say, 'Show us the Father'? Do you not believe that I am in the Father and the Father is in me? The words that I say to you I do not speak on my own authority, but the Father who dwells in me does his works. Believe me that I am in the Father and the Father is in me, or else believe on account of the works themselves.

"Truly, truly, I say to you, whoever believes in me will also do the works that I do; and greater works than these will he do, because I am going to the Father. Whatever you ask in my name, this I will do,

that the Father may be glorified in the Son. If you ask me anything in my name, I will do it.

"If you love me, you will obey my commandments. And I will ask the Father, and he will give you another Helper, to be with you forever, even the Spirit of truth, whom the world cannot receive, because it neither sees him nor knows him. You know him, for he dwells with you and will be in you.

"I will not leave you as orphans; I will come to you. Yet a little while and the world will see me no more, but you will see me. Because I live, you also will live. In that day you will know that I am in my Father, and you in me, and I in you. Whoever has my commandments and keeps them, he it is who loves me. And he who loves me will be loved by my Father, and I will love him and manifest myself to him." Judas (not Iscariot) said to him, "Lord, how is it that you will manifest yourself to us, and not to the world?" Jesus answered him, "If anyone loves me, he will keep my word, and my Father will love him, and we will come to him and make our home with him. Whoever does not love me does not keep my words. And the word that you hear is not mine but the Father's who sent me.

"These things I have spoken to you while I am still with you. But the Helper, the Holy Spirit, whom the Father will send in my name, he will teach and remind all that I have said to you.[34] Peace I leave with you; my peace I give to you. Not as the world gives do I give to you. Let not your hearts be troubled, neither let them be afraid. You heard me say to you, 'I am going away, and I will come to you.' If you loved me, you would have rejoiced, because I am going to the Father, for the Father is greater than I. And now I have told you before it takes place, so that when it does take place you may believe. I will no longer talk much with you, for the ruler of this world is coming. He has no claim on me, but I do as the Father has commanded me, so that the world may know that I love the Father. Rise, let us go from here.

---

[34] The ESV states, "But the Helper, the Holy Spirit, whom the Father will send in my name, he will teach you all things and bring to your remembrance all that I have said to you."

12.0 **What were Jesus and the Disciples doing, and where were they, and what part of the day** (i.e. morning, afternoon, or evening), **was it when He was teaching them in John 13:31 – 14:31** (i.e. what... where... when... note: you may want to compare this event with the synoptic gospels)**?**

13.1 **What is Christ's "new commandment?"**

13.2 **How will "all people know that you are [Jesus'] disciples?"**

14.1 **How does the account of Jesus' telling His disciples, "Where I am going, you cannot come" (John 13:36) differ from the account of when He told the Jews where He was going (John 7:34 and 8:21)?**

14.2 **What did Jesus tell Peter when he confidently said, "I will lay down my life for you?"**

15.1 **What are some reasons why you think Jesus went to His Father's house?**

15.2 **What is the "way" to the Father's house?**

additional notes

Session 11b

16.1 What will "whoever believes" in Jesus be doing?

16.2 Why will Christ do "whatever you ask in [His] name?"

17.0 What will someone do if they love Jesus Christ?

18.1 "In that day" when the Holy Spirit lives in you, who will we "know" is "in" whom (hint: John 14:20)?

18.2 Who will love the person who "has [Jesus'] commandments and keeps them" (hint: John 14:21)?

18.3 What will Jesus Christ do to the one who has and keeps His commandments (i.e. what will happen as a result of loving Jesus Christ through obedience, John 14:21)?

18.4 How did Jesus answer Judas' question in John 14:22?

additional notes

Session 11b

19.1 Who does Jesus say "the Father will send in [His] name"?

19.2 Who does an individual "receive" when they accept anyone sent by Jesus (hint: John 13:20, question 9 of Session 11a)?

19.3 "Whoever accepts" Jesus also "receives" who else (hint: John 13:20, question 9 of Session 11a)?

20.1 What will "the Helper, the Holy Spirit, whom the Father will send in [Jesus'] name," do (note: you may want to refer to the provided translation to help answer this question)?

20.2 Why did Jesus tell His disciples about His departure to the Father "before it takes place"?

20.3 Why will Jesus "no longer talk much" with His disciples? What do you think this means?

20.4 Why do you think the ruler of this world has no claim on Jesus?

20.5 Why does Jesus "do as the Father has commanded" Him?

20.6 So why do you think Jesus voluntarily went to the cross?

additional notes

John 15:1 – 16:4a

"I am the true vine, and my Father is the vinedresser. Every branch in me that does not bear fruit he lifts up, and every branch that does bear fruit he prunes, that it may bear more fruit. You have already been pruned because of the word that I have spoken to you. Live in me, and I in you. As the branch cannot bear fruit by itself, unless it lives in the vine, neither can you, unless you live in me. I am the vine; you are the branches. Whoever lives in me and I in him, he it is that bears much fruit, for apart from me you can do nothing. If anyone does not live in me he is thrown away like a branch and withers; and the branches are gathered, thrown into the fire, and burned. If you live in me, and my words live in you, ask whatever you wish, and it will be done for you. By this my Father is glorified, that you bear much fruit and so prove to be my disciples. As the Father has loved me, so have I loved you. Live in my love. If you keep my commandments, you will live in my love, just as I have kept my Father's commandments and live in his love. These things I have spoken to you, that my joy may be in you, and that your joy may be full.[35]

---

[35] The ESV states, "I am the true vine, and my Father is the vinedresser. Every branch in me that does not bear fruit he takes away, and every branch that does bear fruit he prunes, that it may bear more fruit. Already you are clean because of the word that I have spoken to you. Abide in me, and I in you. As the branch cannot bear fruit by itself, unless it abides in the vine, neither can you, unless you abide in me. I am the vine; you are the branches. Whoever abides in me and I in him, he it is that bears much fruit, for apart from me you can do nothing. If anyone does not abide in me he is thrown away like a branch and withers; and the branches are gathered, thrown into the fire, and burned. If you abide in me, and my words abide in you, ask whatever you wish, and it will be done for you. By this my Father is glorified, that you bear much fruit and so prove to be my disciples. As the Father has loved me, so have I loved you. Abide in my love. If you keep my commandments, you will abide in my love, just as I have kept my Father's commandments and abide in his love. These things I have spoken to you, that my joy may be in you, and that your joy may be full."

John 15:1 – 16:4a

"This is my commandment, that you love one another as I have loved you. Greater love has no one than this, that someone lay down his life for his friends. You are my friends if you do what I command you. No longer do I call you servants, for the servant does not know what his master is doing; but I have called you friends, for all that I have heard from my Father I have made known to you. You did not choose me, but I chose you and appointed you that you should go and bear fruit and that your fruit should live, so that whatever you ask the Father in my name, he may give it to you.[36] These things I command you, so that you will love one another.

"If the world hates you, know that it has hated me before it hated you. If you were of the world, the world would love you as its own; but because you are not of the world, but I chose you out of the world, therefore the world hates you. Remember the word that I said to you: 'A servant is not greater than his master.' If they persecuted me, they will also persecute you. If they kept my word, they will also keep yours. But all these things they will do to you on account of my name, because they do not know him who sent me. If I had not come and spoken to them, they would not have been guilty of sin, but now they have no excuse for their sin. Whoever hates me hates my Father also. If I had not done among them the works that no one else did, they would not be guilty of sin, but now they have seen and hated both me and my Father. But the word that is written in their Law must be fulfilled: 'They hated me without a cause.'

"But when the Helper comes, whom I will send to you from the Father, the Spirit of truth, who proceeds from the Father, he will bear witness about me. And you also will bear witness, because you have been with me from the beginning.

---

[36] The ESV states, "You did not choose me, but I chose you and appointed you that you should go and bear fruit and that your fruit should abide, so that whatever you ask the Father in my name, he may give it to you."

"I have said all these things to you to keep you from falling away. They will put you out of the synagogues. Indeed, the hour is coming when whoever kills you will think he is offering service to God. And they will do these things because they have not known the Father, nor me. But I have said these things to you, that when their hour comes you may remember that I told them to you.

An article on "The Vine"

"The common grapevine is mentioned in Scripture from the time of Noah. The *Vitas vinifera* (Latin) may have been native to northern Persia, but its origin is very obscure. A characteristic product of the Promised Land, it became an important item of the Hebrew economy (Dt. 8:8; cf. 6:11; Josh. 24:13; Neh. 9:25); wine represents one of God's best gifts to human beings (Jgs. 9:13; Ps. 104:15). Jacob's blessing on Judah shows the suitability of the latter's portion of the land for cultivating vines (Gen. 49:11f.). During the captivity the poor were left behind as vinedressers and plowmen (2 K. 25:12; Jer. 52:16) lest the land become completely desolate. When the captives returned, however this duty would fall to "foreigners" (Isa. 61:5).

"Viticulture has always been prominent in the hill country of Samaria and Judea where the natural contours provide excellent terraces (cf. Isa. 5:1f.). In early days the vine lay along the ground or trailed over walls and rocks (cf. Gen. 49:22), but later it was supported by poles or trellises (cf. 1 K. 4:25; Mic. 4:4; Zec. 3:10). Constant care was necessary to ensure a fruitful vine. After the rains

any damage to the terraces was repaired, and the ground was dug and cleared of weeds. Because of the delicate structure and of the vine, damage was easily sustained by the plant, whether from storms, animal depredations, or the destruction caused by trespassers or pillagers. Fallen vines were lifted into position with meticulous care and allowed to heal **(Jn 15:2, *airei*, from *airō*, "to lift up," <u>not</u> from *airéō*, 'to cut off, take away,' as in all English Versions)**.

"As in other plants, the quality of the fruit was safeguarded by the pruning of the branches. This operation was performed with pruning hooks (Heb. *mazmērôṯ*, Isa. 2:4; 18:5; Joel 3:10; Mic. 4:3), which were small sickle-shaped knives that may have been weapons originally, and could certainly be converted to such purposes quickly were an enemy attack to threaten. Dead branches were pruned in spring (Lev. 25:3f.; Isa. 5:6) and were gathered for burning (Jn. 15:6). Foxes and jackal menaced the ripening grapes (Cant. 2:15), and in some districts wild boars damaged growing vines (Ps. 30:8, 12f. [NT9, 13f.]). In the vineyards one or more stone towers were erected, in which the vinedressers lived (Isa. 5:2; Nt. 21:33 par. Mk. 12:1)."[37]

The main vine is the source of life for the branches. Life giving nutrition and sap flows to the branches from the vine. The only way the branches can live is if they have a healthy connection to the vine. If a branch were to fall to the ground from the trellises, it is in grave danger. The branch may not get the sunlight or air it properly needs. Secondly, a fallen branch left on the ground is more vulnerable to predators, pestilence, and diseases than if it were lifted back up onto the trellises. Any of these negative influences would prevent the branch from reaching its fruit producing potential. And finally, and maybe most importantly, if the branch were to fall off the trellises, it could become kinked where it is connected to the vine. This could prevent the life giving sap of the vine from flowing into the delicate branch, causing it to wither and even potentially die.

---

[37] The International Standard Bible Encyclopedia, Vol. IV, page 986

A competent gardener/vinedresser would quickly and gently lift up a fallen branch. Not only would a vinedresser lift up and nurture fallen branches, he would also tend to the healthier branches. The greatest fruit is produced on the end of the branches. The vinedresser would gently prune the sucker leaves and little shoots off the branches. This would allow more of the life giving sap to flow to the areas of the branch most needed to produce abundant fruit. The production and life of the branches (i.e. believers) are completely dependent on the nutrition of a healthy vine (i.e. Christ) and the attentive care of a competent vinedresser (i.e. the Father). Any branch that is not in the vine will dry up and be collected for burning (i.e. an unbeliever). Apart from the vine, the branch can do nothing. And for any branch to reach its full fruit producing potential, it is dependent on the vinedresser's protection, pruning, and assiduous care.

An article on *airō* (to lift up)

John clearly uses the word *airō* in his original Greek manuscript. The definition of the word *airō* is also not disputed. The following is the primary definition for *airō* as found in a Koinē Greek New Testament Theological Dictionary:

"*airō* (to lift up, to lift up in order to carry off), *epairō* (to lift up). *airō*. The meanings are 'to lift from the ground,' 'to lift in order to carry,' and 'to carry off.'

1. The sense 'to lift up' occurs for raising the hand in an oath (Rev. 10:5), rising the face in prayer (Jn. 11:41), and raising the voice in prayer (Acts 4:24), [and to lift up a fallen branch (John 15:2)].[38]

---

[38] Theological Dictionary of the New Testament, Abridged one Volume, pages 28-29

It is undeniably clear on what Greek word was penned by John and what this Greek word means. The real question is how and why English translators have commonly mistranslated this Greek word in John 15:2. The main explanation is cradled in long traditional presuppositions existing from heretical theological persuasions. The Roman Catholic Church leveraged their authority by equating being cut off from the grace of Christ with excommunication from the Church. This tactical abusive stance manipulated compliance of the parishioners through fear. Many cults have followed suit. This manipulative teaching, often utilizing the passage of John 15, has been instilled for over a millennium before translators first translated this passage into English. Since the first complete English translation in A.D. 1611, nearly every other English translation has since conformed.

In the John 15 passage there are two types of branches; the first kind of branch has three subcategories. The two kinds of branches are: the branches "in Christ" (v. 2); and the branches that "are not in Christ" (v.6). The branches that are not in Christ are spiritually dead unbelievers. The branches that are in Christ are believers that are spiritually living as one with Christ. "Most exegetes understand [the vine or vine stalk] to include both stalk and branches, since the branches can be regarded as part of the vine, in the same way that believers may be regarded as part of Christ; that is, they are in him even as he is in them."[39] Every believer (i.e. those that are in Christ) goes through stages in their lives when they are more fruitful than others. There are three categories of branches that are living in the vine: 1). those that are presently not producing fruit; 2). those that are bearing fruit but should bear more; 3). and those that are bearing much fruit. Believers have been grafted into the perfect vine and the Father is a masterful vinedresser that knows how to nurture his branches to maximize the desired fruit production at just the right time in order to accomplish His desired purpose.

---

[39] Newman, B. M., & Nida, E. A. (1993). A handbook on the Gospel of John. UBS Handbook Series (479). New York: United Bible Societies.

Short Answer: John 15:1 – 16:4a. Answer the following questions pertaining based on the above articles and John chapter 15. Write the reference (chapter and verse) that best supports your answer (note: all questions and quotes are taken from the ESV translation).

21.0 **What do you think the Disciples understood when Jesus said, "I am the true vine" in John 15:1** (hint: you may want to read the following passages to help better answer this question: Psalm 80:8-18; Isaiah 3:14, 5:1-7; Jeremiah 2:21, 12:10; Ezekiel 15:1-5, 17:5-10, 19:10-14; and Hosea 10:1.)**?**

22.1 **What is the vinedresser's goal for the branches?**

22.2 **According to the context of John 15, along with the previous articles, what is the most accurate way to translate John 15:2?**

"Every branch in me that does not bear fruit he _____ _____..."

22.3 **How could the "takes away" in John 15:2 of the ESV translation be misinterpreted?**

22.4 **How could this action of lifting up a branch, help the branch that is not producing fruit to become fruitful** (note: you may want to refer to the provided translation and articles to help correctly answer this question)**?**

22.5 **What does the vinedresser do with the branches that are producing fruit?**

22.6 **Why would He do this?**

additional notes

22.7 **What do you think God uses to spiritually "prune" His branches so they will produce more fruit** (note: you may want to refer to the ESV Study Bible Notes along with John 15:3 with Ephesians 5:26)**?**

22.8 **What do you think it means to "bear fruit"** (note: you may want refer to the ESV Study Bible Notes, cross-references, and consider what the fruit was used for)**?**

22.9 **In the allegory found in John 15:1-7 what do you think each of the following represent: the Father; the object that represents Christ; the branch in the vine that bears much fruit; the branch in the vine that bears some fruit; the branch in the vine that does not bear fruit; and the branch not in the vine that is thrown in the fire?**

23.1 **What commandment did Jesus say "is my commandment"?**

23.2 **What is the "greatest love" someone could have for someone else?**

23.3 **What is the difference between a "servant" and a "friend"?**

23.4 **What has Jesus "made known" to us?**

additional notes

23.5 **Why do you think He has made this known to us** (hint: you may want to refer back to Session 6, question 7 and reflect on why the Father made it known to Jesus along with John 15:16-17)**?**

23.6 **Did we choose Jesus or did Jesus choose us? Explain.**

24.0 **List at least three reasons why the world hates Christians.**

25.1 **Who will Jesus send to whom from whom?**

25.2 **According to verse 26, what is another name for the Helper?**

25.3 **What will the Person who was sent by Christ from the Father do?**

25.4 **Why will people treat Jesus' disciples so harshly, even to the point of wanting to kill them?**

additional notes

John 16:4b – 17:26

"I did not say these things to you from the beginning, because I was with you. But now I am going to him who sent me, and none of you asks me, 'Where are you going?' But because I have said these things to you, sorrow has filled your heart. Nevertheless, I tell you the truth: it is to your advantage that I go away, for if I do not go away, the Helper will not come to you. But if I go, I will send him to you. And when he comes, he will convict the world concerning sin and righteousness and judgment: concerning sin, because they do not believe in me; concerning righteousness, because I go to the Father, and you will see me no longer; concerning judgment, because the ruler of this world is judged.

"I still have many things to say to you, but you cannot bear them now. When the Spirit of truth comes, he will guide you into all the truth, for he will not speak on his own authority, but whatever he hears he will speak, and he will declare to you the things that are to come.

He will glorify me, for he will take what is mine and declare it to you. All that the Father has is mine; therefore I said that he will take what is mine and declare it to you.

"A little while, and you will see me no longer; and again a little while, and you will see me." So some of his disciples said to one another, "What is this that he says to us, 'A little while, and you will not see me, and again a little while, and you will see me'; and, 'because I am going to the Father'?" So they were saying, "What does he mean by 'a little while'? We do not know what he is talking about." Jesus knew that they wanted to ask him, so he said to them, "Is this what you are asking yourselves, what I meant by saying, 'A little while and you will not see me, and again a little while and you will see me'? Truly, truly, I say to you, you will weep and lament, but the world will rejoice. You will be sorrowful, but your sorrow will turn into joy. When a woman is giving birth, she has sorrow because her hour has come, but when she has delivered the baby, she no longer

remembers the anguish, for joy that a human being has been born into the world. So also you have sorrow now, but I will see you again, and your hearts will rejoice, and no one will take your joy from you. In that day you will ask nothing of me. Truly, truly, I say to you, whatever you ask of the Father in my name, he will give it to you. Until now you have asked nothing in my name. Ask, and you will receive, that your joy may be full.

"I have said these things to you in figures of speech. The hour is coming when I will no longer speak to you in figures of speech but will tell you plainly about the Father. In that day you will ask in my name, and I do not say to you that I will ask the Father on your behalf; for the Father himself loves you, because you have loved me and have believed that I came from God. I came from the Father and have come into the world, and now I am leaving the world and going to the Father."

His disciples said, "Ah, now you are speaking plainly and not using figurative speech! Now we know that you know all things and do not need anyone to question you; this is why we believe that you came from God." Jesus answered them, "Do you now believe? Behold, the hour is coming, indeed it has come, when you will be scattered, each to his own home, and will leave me alone. Yet I am not alone, for the Father is with me. I have said these things to you, that in me you may have peace. In the world you will have tribulation. But take heart; I have overcome the world."

When Jesus had spoken these words, he lifted up his eyes to heaven, and said, "Father, the hour has come; glorify your Son that the Son may glorify you, since you have given him authority over all flesh, to give eternal life to all whom you have given him. And this is eternal life, that they know you the only true God, and Jesus Christ whom you have sent. I glorified you on earth, having accomplished the work that you gave me to do. And now, Father, glorify me in your

own presence with the glory that I had with you before the world existed.

"I have manifested your name to the people whom you gave me out of the world. Yours they were, and you gave them to me, and they have kept your word. Now they know that everything that you have given me is from you. For I have given them the words that you gave me, and they have received them and have come to know in truth that I came from you; and they have believed that you sent me. I am praying for them. I am not praying for the world but for those whom you have given me, for they are yours. All mine are yours, and yours are mine, and I am glorified in them. And I am no longer in the world, but they are in the world, and I am coming to you. Holy Father, keep them in your name, which you have given me, that they may be one, even as we are one. While I was with them, I kept them in your name, which you have given me. I have guarded them, and not one of them has been lost except the son of destruction, that the Scripture might be fulfilled. But now I am coming to you, and these things I speak in the world, that they may have my joy fulfilled in themselves. I have given them your word, and the world has hated them because they are not of the world, just as I am not of the world. I do not ask that you take them out of the world, but that you keep them from the evil one. They are not of the world, just as I am not of the world.

Sanctify them in the truth; your word is truth. As you sent me into the world, so I have sent them into the world. And for their sake I sanctify myself, that they also may be sanctified in truth.

"I do not ask for these only, but also for those who will believe in me through their word, that they may all be one, just as you, Father, are in me, and I in you, that they also may be in us, so that the world may believe that you have sent me. The glory that you have given me I have given to them, that they may be one even as we are one, I in them and you in me, that they may become perfectly one, so that the world may know that you sent me and loved them even as

you loved me. Father, I desire that they also, whom you have given me, may be with me where I am, to see my glory that you have given me because you loved me before the foundation of the world. O righteous Father, even though the world does not know you, I know you, and these know that you have sent me. I made known to them your name, and I will continue to make it known, that the love with which you have loved me may be in them, and I in them."

additional notes

Session 11d

26.1 Who will come when Jesus goes away?

26.2 What three ways will He "convict" the world? Explain what you think each of these three mean.

27.1 According to John 16:12-15, what will the "Spirit of truth" do when He comes and what will this do (note: you may want to refer back to Session 11c, question 25.3)**?**

27.2 **How do you think He will do this** (note: you may want to refer back to Session 11b, question 20.1 and Session 11c, question 25.3)**?**

28.0 Why does "the Father Himself love you"?

29.0 Why has Jesus "said these things to you"?

30.0 What is "eternal life"? **Explain** (note: you may want to cross-reference eternal life and read the corresponding ESV Study Bible Notes)**.**

additional notes

Session 11d

31.1 How has Jesus Christ "glorified [the Father] on earth"?

31.2 With what kind of glory, and where does Jesus want, the Father to glorify Him?

31.3 What is the "work" that Jesus has "completed" (you may want to refer to Session 5, question 6 and Session 7, question 5 along with their corresponding verses)?

32.1 In John 17:6, what does it mean to "manifest" one's name (note: you may want to refer to the ESV Study Bible Notes)?

32.2 What is God's name (This answer is not necessarily found within our immediate text. Note: you may want to refer to Matthew 28:16-20 and consider the Name in which someone is baptized)?

33.1 What does "sanctify" mean (note: you may want to refer to the ESV foot note)?

33.2 What is it that sanctifies the believer?

33.3 What is truth?

additional notes

Session 11d

Short Answer: John 16:04b-17:26. Write the reference (chapter and verse) that best supports your answer (note: all questions and quotes are taken from the ESV translation).

34.0 Why do you think God does not rapture a believer (i.e. take us to heaven) out of this world immediately after conversion?

35.1 In what like manner have believers been "sent into the world?"

35.2 Why did Jesus consecrate/sanctify himself?

35.3 What do you think it means that Jesus sanctified himself?

36.1 Why has Christ given us the glory that the Father gave him?

36.2 What do Christians being "perfectly one" accomplish?

37.0 When praying to the Father about His Disciples, why did Christ say He has "made known to them [the Father's] name, and will continue to make it known?"

additional notes

Session 12

John 18:1 – 19:16a

When Jesus had spoken these words, he went out with his disciples across the brook Kidron, where there was a garden, which he and his disciples entered. Now Judas, who betrayed him, also knew the place, for Jesus often met there with his disciples. So Judas, having procured a band of soldiers and some officers from the chief priests and the Pharisees, went there with lanterns and torches and weapons. Then Jesus, knowing all that would happen to him, came forward and said to them, "Whom do you seek?" They answered him, "Jesus of Nazareth." Jesus said to them, "I AM." Judas, who betrayed him, was standing with them. When Jesus said to them, "I AM," they drew back and fell to the ground. So he asked them again, "Whom do you seek?" And they said, "Jesus of Nazareth." Jesus answered, "I told you that I AM. So, if you seek me, let these men go."[40] This was to fulfill the word that he had spoken: "Of those whom you gave me I have lost not one." Then Simon Peter, having a sword, drew it and struck the high priest's servant and cut off his right ear. (The servant's name was Malchus.) So Jesus said to Peter, "Put your sword into its sheath; shall I not drink the cup that the Father has given me?"

So the band of soldiers and their captain and the officers of the Jews arrested Jesus and bound him. First they led him to Annas, for he was the father-in-law of Caiaphas, who was high priest that year. It was Caiaphas who had advised the Jews that it would be expedient that one man should die for the people.

Simon Peter followed Jesus, and so did another disciple. Since that disciple was known to the high priest, he entered with Jesus into the courtyard of the high priest, but Peter stood outside at the door.

---

[40] The ESV states, "They answered him, "Jesus of Nazareth." Jesus said to them, "I am he." Judas, who betrayed him, was standing with them. When Jesus said to them, "I am he," they drew back and fell to the ground. So he asked them again, "Whom do you seek?" And they said, "Jesus of Nazareth." Jesus answered, "I told you that I am he. So, if you seek me, let these men go."

So the other disciple, who was known to the high priest, went out and spoke to the servant girl who kept watch at the door, and brought Peter in. The servant girl at the door said to Peter, "You're not one of this man's disciples, are you?" He said, "I am not." Now the servants and officers had made a charcoal fire, because it was cold, and they were standing and warming themselves. Peter also was with them, standing and warming himself.

The high priest then questioned Jesus about his disciples and his teaching. Jesus answered him, "I have spoken openly to the world. I have always taught in synagogues and in the temple, where all Jews come together. I have said nothing in secret. Why do you ask me? Ask those who have heard me what I said to them; they know what I said." When he had said these things, one of the officers standing by struck Jesus with his hand, saying, "Is that how you answer the high priest?" Jesus answered him, "If what I said is wrong, bear witness about the wrong; but if what I said is right, why do you strike me?" Annas then sent him bound to Caiaphas the high priest.

Now Simon Peter was standing and warming himself. So they said to him, "You're not one of his disciples, are you?" He denied it and said, "I am not." One of the servants of the high priest, a relative of the man whose ear Peter had cut off, asked, "I saw you in the garden with Jesus, didn't I?"[41] Peter again denied it, and at once a rooster crowed.

Then they led Jesus from the house of Caiaphas to the governor's headquarters. It was early morning. They themselves did not enter the governor's headquarters, so that they would not be defiled, but could eat the Passover. So Pilate went outside to them and said, "What accusation do you bring against this man?" They answered him, "If this man were not doing evil, we would not have delivered him over to you." Pilate said to them, "Take him yourselves

---

[41] The ESV states, "One of the servants of the high priest, a relative of the man whose ear Peter had cut off, asked, 'Did I not see you in the garden with him?'"

and judge him by your own law." The Jews said to him, "It is not lawful for us to put anyone to death." This was to fulfill the word that Jesus had spoken to show by what kind of death he was going to die.

So Pilate entered his headquarters again and called Jesus and said to him, "Are you the King of the Jews?" Jesus answered, "Do you say this of your own accord, or did others say it to you about me?" Pilate answered, "Am I a Jew? Your own nation and the chief priests have delivered you over to me. What have you done?" Jesus answered, "My kingdom is not of this world. If my kingdom were of this world, my servants would have been fighting, that I might not be delivered over to the Jews. But my kingdom is not from the world." Then Pilate said to him, "So you are a king?" Jesus answered, "You say that I am a king. For this purpose I was born and for this purpose I have come into the world—to bear witness to the truth. Everyone who is of the truth listens to my voice." Pilate said to him, "What is truth?"

After he had said this, he went back outside to the Jews and told them, "I find no guilt in him. But you have a custom that I should release one man for you at the Passover. So do you want me to release to you the King of the Jews?" They cried out again, "Not this man, but Barabbas!" Now Barabbas was a robber.

Then Pilate took Jesus and flogged him. And the soldiers twisted together a crown of thorns and put it on his head and arrayed him in a purple robe. They came up to him, saying, "Hail, King of the Jews!" and struck him with their hands. Pilate went out again and said to them, "See, I am bringing him out to you that you may know that I find no guilt in him." So Jesus came out, wearing the crown of thorns and the purple robe. Pilate said to them, "Behold the man!" When the chief priests and the officers saw him, they cried out, "Crucify him, crucify him!" Pilate said to them, "Take him yourselves and crucify him, for I find no guilt in him." The Jews answered him, "We have a law, and according to that law he ought to die because he has

made himself the Son of God." When Pilate heard this statement, he was even more afraid. He entered his headquarters again and said to Jesus, "Where are you from?" But Jesus gave him no answer. So Pilate said to him, "You will not speak to me? Do you not know that I have authority to release you and authority to crucify you?" Jesus answered him, "You would have no authority over me at all unless it had been given you from above. Therefore he who delivered me over to you has the greater sin."

From then on Pilate sought to release him, but the Jews cried out, "If you release this man, you are not Caesar's friend. Everyone who makes himself a king opposes Caesar." So when Pilate heard these words, he brought Jesus out and sat down on the judgment seat at a place called The Stone Pavement, and in Aramaic Gabbatha. Now it was the day of Preparation of the Passover. It was about the sixth hour. He said to the Jews, "Behold your King!" They cried out, "Away with him, away with him, crucify him!" Pilate said to them, "Shall I crucify your King?" The chief priests answered, "We have no king but Caesar." So he delivered him over to them to be crucified.

Session 12

1.0 **Where is the Kidron Valley located in respect to Jerusalem** (note: you may want to look for the Kidron Valley on the map located in the ESV Study Bible Notes)**?**

2.1 **How many soldiers did Judas guide to Jesus** (note: a "band of soldiers" was probably a cohort. Look up the ESV Study Bible Notes of Acts 10:1 in the ESV Study Bible)**?**

2.2 **What did the soldiers do when Jesus identified Himself as the "I AM"?**

2.3 **What do you think caused the soldiers to do this** (hint: you may want to refer to the provided translation as well as the chart, "Jesus' 'I Am' Statements" located at the bottom in the ESV Study Bible Notes of John chapter nine)**?**

3.1 **Why do you think Jesus instructed Peter, "Put your sword away!"** (note: you may want to consider Jesus and Pilate's conversation in John 18:36 and what Jesus said about His kingdom)**?**

3.2 **What was the name of the man who had his ear cut off by Peter?**

3.3 **What position did this man's relative also hold?**

4.0 **From the way the questions were asked, what answer was anticipated in each of the following leading questions:** (note: you may want to refer to the provided translation help answer this question)**?**

John 18:17:	❏ Yes	❏ No
John 18:25:	❏ Yes	❏ No
John 18:26:	❏ Yes	❏ No

additional notes

Session 12

5.0   Why did the Jews not enter "the governor's headquarters?"

6.1   What Roman "crime" do you think the Jews accused Jesus of violating?

6.2   What did Jesus do/say throughout the book of John that made the Jews accuse Him of this in John 19:7?

6.3   What did Jesus do/say that made the Jews accuse Him of this?

7.1   What method of execution did the Jews use to inflict the death penalty (hint: you may want to refer to the ESV Study Bible Notes for John 19:6)?

7.2   What method of execution did the Romans use for foreigners and slaves to inflict the death penalty?

7.3   Why do you think the Jews wanted Jesus to be crucified instead of them stoning Him?

8.1   In what ways did Pilate try to free Jesus?

8.2   Why do you think he eventually gave into the Jews?

additional notes

Session 12

The arrest of Jesus and examination by the High Priest: John 18:1-27

<u>event</u>   <u>chapter</u>   <u>verses</u>

1. __G__ , __18__ : __1__ - __3__   A. Peter's first denial of Jesus

2. _____ , ____ : ____ - ____   B. Peter attempts to defend Jesus

3. _____ , ____ : ____ - ____   C. Jesus arrested and led to Annas

4. _____ , ____ : ____ - ____   D. Jesus identifies himself to the Jewish officials and soldiers

5. _____ , ____ : ____ - ____   E. Peter denies Jesus twice more

6. _____ , ____ : ____ - ____   F. Jesus is led to the High Priest

7. _____ , ____ : ____ - ____   G. Judas leads a band of soldiers to arrest Jesus

158

additional notes

The trial of Jesus before Pilate: John 18:28 – 19:16a

<u>event</u> <u>chapter</u>   <u>verses</u>

1. _____, ____ : ____ - ____   A. Pilate's second interrogation

2. _____, ____ : ____ - ____   B. Jesus is flogged and mocked
                                   by soldiers

3. _____, ____ : ____ - ____   C. Jesus is handed over to Pilate

4. _____, ____ : ____ - ____   D. The Jews demanded Jesus to
                                   be crucified and Pilate yields

5. _____, ____ : ____ - ____   E. Pilate's first interrogation and
                                   attempt to release Jesus

6. _____, ____ : ____ - ____   F. Pilate's final attempt to release
                                   Jesus as the King of the Jews

7. _____, ____ : ____ - ____   G. Jesus is declared innocent,
                                   presented, and mocked as a king

additional notes

So they took Jesus, and he went out, bearing his own cross, to the place called The Place of a Skull, which in Aramaic is called Golgotha. There they crucified him, and with him two others, one on either side, and Jesus between them. Pilate also wrote an inscription and put it on the cross. It read, "Jesus of Nazareth, the King of the Jews." Many of the Jews read this inscription, for the place where Jesus was crucified was near the city, and it was written in Aramaic, in Latin, and in Greek. So the chief priests of the Jews said to Pilate, "Do not write, 'The King of the Jews,' but rather, 'This man said, I am King of the Jews.'" Pilate answered, "What I have written I have written."

When the soldiers had crucified Jesus, they took his garments and divided them into four parts, one part for each soldier; also his tunic. But the tunic was seamless, woven in one piece from top to bottom, so they said to one another, "Let us not tear it, but cast lots for it to see whose it shall be." This was to fulfill the Scripture which says, "They divided my garments among them, and for my clothing they cast lots." So the soldiers did these things, but standing by the cross of Jesus were his mother and his mother's sister, Mary the wife of Clopas, and Mary Magdalene. When Jesus saw his mother and the disciple whom he loved standing nearby, he said to his mother, "Woman, behold, your son!" Then he said to the disciple, "Behold, your mother!" And from that hour the disciple took her to his own home.

After this, Jesus, knowing that all was now finished, said (to fulfill the Scripture), "I thirst." A jar full of sour wine stood there, so they put a sponge full of the sour wine on a hyssop branch and held it to his mouth. When Jesus had received the sour wine, he said, "It is finished," and he bowed his head and gave up his spirit.

Since it was the day of Preparation, and so that the bodies would not remain on the cross on the Sabbath (for that Sabbath was a high day), the Jews asked Pilate that their legs might be broken and

that they might be taken away. So the soldiers came and broke the legs of the first, and of the other who had been crucified with him. But when they came to Jesus and saw that he was already dead, they did not break his legs. But one of the soldiers pierced his side with a spear, and at once there came out blood and water. He who saw it has borne witness—his testimony is true, and he knows that he is telling the truth—that you also may believe. For these things took place that the Scripture might be fulfilled: "Not one of his bones will be broken." And again another Scripture says, "They will look on him whom they have pierced."

After these things Joseph of Arimathea, who was a disciple of Jesus, but secretly for fear of the Jews, asked Pilate that he might take away the body of Jesus, and Pilate gave him permission. So he came and took away his body. Nicodemus also, who earlier had come to Jesus by night, came bringing a mixture of myrrh and aloes, about seventy-five pounds in weight. So they took the body of Jesus and bound it in linen cloths with the spices, as is the burial custom of the Jews. Now in the place where he was crucified there was a garden, and in the garden a new tomb in which no one had yet been laid. So because of the Jewish day of Preparation, since the tomb was close at hand, they laid Jesus there.

Now on the first day of the week Mary Magdalene came to the tomb early, while it was still dark, and saw that the stone had been taken away from the tomb. So she ran and went to Simon Peter and the other disciple, the one whom Jesus loved, and said to them, "They have taken the Lord out of the tomb, and we do not know where they have laid him." So Peter went out with the other disciple, and they were going toward the tomb. Both of them were running together, but the other disciple outran Peter and reached the tomb first. And stooping to look in, he saw the linen cloths lying there, but he did not go in. Then Simon Peter came, following him, and went into the tomb. He saw the linen cloths lying there, and the face cloth, which

had been on Jesus' head, not lying with the linen cloths but folded up in a place by itself. Then the other disciple, who had reached the tomb first, also went in, and he saw and believed; for as yet they did not understand the Scripture, that he must rise from the dead. Then the disciples went back to their homes.

But Mary stood weeping outside the tomb, and as she wept she stooped to look into the tomb. And she saw two angels in white, sitting where the body of Jesus had lain, one at the head and one at the feet. They said to her, "Woman, why are you weeping?" She said to them, "They have taken away my Lord, and I do not know where they have laid him." Having said this, she turned around and saw Jesus standing, but she did not know that it was Jesus. Jesus said to her, "Woman, why are you weeping? Whom are you seeking?" Supposing him to be the gardener, she said to him, "Sir, if you have carried him away, tell me where you have laid him, and I will take him away." Jesus said to her, "Mary." She turned and said to him in Aramaic, "Rabboni!" (which means Teacher). Jesus said to her, "Do not cling to me, for I have not yet ascended to the Father; but go to my brothers and say to them, 'I am ascending to my Father and your Father, to my God and your God.'" Mary Magdalene went and announced to the disciples, "I have seen the Lord"—and that he had said these things to her.

On the evening of that day, the first day of the week, the doors being locked where the disciples were for fear of the Jews, Jesus came and stood among them and said to them, "Peace be with you." When he had said this, he showed them his hands and his side. Then the disciples were glad when they saw the Lord. Jesus said to them again, "Peace be with you. As the Father has sent me, even so I am sending you." And when he had said this, he breathed on them and said to them, "Receive the Holy Spirit. If you forgive the sins of any, they are forgiven them; if you withhold forgiveness from any, it is withheld."

Now Thomas, one of the Twelve, called the Twin, was not with them when Jesus came. So the other disciples told him, "We have seen the Lord." But he said to them, "Unless I see in his hands the mark of the nails, and place my finger into the mark of the nails, and place my hand into his side, I will never believe."

Eight days later, his disciples were inside again, and Thomas was with them. Although the doors were locked, Jesus came and stood among them and said, "Peace be with you." Then he said to Thomas, "Put your finger here, and see my hands; and put out your hand, and place it in my side. Do not disbelieve, but believe." Thomas answered him, "My Lord and my God!" Jesus said to him, "Have you believed because you have seen me? Blessed are those who have not seen and yet have believed."

Now Jesus did many other signs in the presence of the disciples, which are not written in this book; but these are written so that you may believe that Jesus is the Christ, the Son of God, and that by believing you may have life in his name.

After this Jesus revealed himself again to the disciples by the Sea of Tiberias, and he revealed himself in this way. Simon Peter, Thomas (called the Twin), Nathanael of Cana in Galilee, the sons of Zebedee, and two others of his disciples were together. Simon Peter said to them, "I am going fishing." They said to him, "We will go with you." They went out and got into the boat, but that night they caught nothing.

Just as day was breaking, Jesus stood on the shore; yet the disciples did not know that it was Jesus. Jesus said to them, "Children, do you have any fish?" They answered him, "No." He said to them, "Cast the net on the right side of the boat, and you will find some." So they cast it, and now they were not able to haul it in, because of the quantity of fish. That disciple whom Jesus loved therefore said to Peter, "It is the Lord!" When Simon Peter heard that it was the Lord, he put on his outer garment, for he was stripped for work, and threw

himself into the sea. The other disciples came in the boat, dragging the net full of fish, for they were not far from the land, but about a hundred yards off.

When they got out on land, they saw a charcoal fire in place, with fish laid out on it, and bread. Jesus said to them, "Bring some of the fish that you have just caught." So Simon Peter went aboard and hauled the net ashore, full of large fish, 153 of them. And although there were so many, the net was not torn. Jesus said to them, "Come and have breakfast." Now none of the disciples dared ask him, "Who are you?" They knew it was the Lord. Jesus came and took the bread and gave it to them, and so with the fish. This was now the third time that Jesus was revealed to the disciples after he was raised from the dead.

When they had finished breakfast, Jesus said to Simon Peter, "Simon, son of John, do you love me more than these?" He said to him, "Yes, Lord; you know that I love you." He said to him, "Feed my lambs." He said to him a second time, "Simon, son of John, do you love me?" He said to him, "Yes, Lord; you know that I love you." He said to him, "Tend my sheep." He said to him the third time, "Simon, son of John, do you love me?" Peter was grieved because he said to him the third time, "Do you love me?" and he said to him, "Lord, you know everything; you know that I love you." Jesus said to him, "Feed my sheep. Truly, truly, I say to you, when you were young, you used to dress yourself and walk wherever you wanted, but when you are old, you will stretch out your hands, and another will dress you and carry you where you do not want to go." (This he said to show by what kind of death he was to glorify God.) And after saying this he said to him, "Follow me."

Peter turned and saw the disciple whom Jesus loved following them, the one who also had leaned back against him during the supper and had said, "Lord, who is it that is going to betray you?"

When Peter saw him, he said to Jesus, "Lord, what about this man?" Jesus said to him, "If it is my will that he remain until I come, what is that to you? You follow me!" So the saying spread abroad among the brothers that this disciple was not to die; yet Jesus did not say to him that he was not to die, but, "If it is my will that he remain until I come, what is that to you?"

This is the disciple who is bearing witness about these things, and who has written these things, and we know that his testimony is true.

Now there are also many other things that Jesus did. Were every one of them to be written, I suppose that the world itself could not contain the books that would be written.

Session 13

1.1   Why do you think Pilate had "Jesus of Nazareth, King of the Jews" written in Aramaic, Latin, and Greek (note: you may want to refer to the ESV Study Bible Notes)?

1.2   How could "many of the Jews read this inscription" even though many of them did not live in or near Jerusalem (John 19:20)?

2.1   What do you think Jesus meant when He said, "It is finished" (note: you may want to refer to the ESV Study Bible Notes)?

2.2   What do you think caused Jesus' body to expire (hint: you may want to cross-reference "gave up his spirit" in John 19:30 and look up James 2:26)?

3.1   What "Jewish day" was it when Jesus died?

3.2   What was the next day going to be?

3.3   What does "high day" or special Sabbath mean (note: you may want to refer to the ESV Study Bible Notes)?

3.4   What time of day was it when Jesus died (hint: you may want to refer to the crucifixion account in Matthew 27:45)?

4.0   How did smashing the legs with a large mallet of a person being crucified expedite the death process (note: you may want to refer to the ESV Study Bible Notes)?

additional notes

Session 13

5.1   How long do you think Jesus had been raised from the dead until most of His disciples first saw Him?

5.2   How many appearances of Jesus does Scripture record between His resurrection to His ascension (note: you may want to refer to ESV Study Bible Notes of John 20:6 and cross-references. You may also want to look up "appeared" in the Concordance and read the paragraph of the 1 Corinthians reference. You can also refer to the chart on the following page)?

6.1   What did Jesus tell Mary Magdalene to go and tell His disciples?

6.2   What did Thomas say when Jesus told him to, "Do not disbelieve, but believe?"

6.3   Who is "blessed" for their belief?

7.1   Does Scripture record all the miracles of Jesus?

7.2   Why have some of the miraculous signs of Jesus been written down and recorded?

7.3   If everything were "written" that Jesus had done, how many books would be written?

Resurrection Appearances

Event	Matt	Mark	Luke	John	Acts	1 Cor.
At the empty tomb outside Jerusalem	28:1-10	16:1-8	24:1-12	20:1-9		
To Mary Magdalene at the tomb		16:9-11		20:11-18		
To two travelers on the road to Emmaus			24:13-32			
To Peter in Jerusalem			24:34			15:5
To the ten disciples in the upper room		16:14	24:36-43	20:19-25		
To the eleven disciples in the upper room				20:26-31		
To seven disciples fishing on the Sea of Galilee				21:1-23		
To the eleven disciples on the mountain in Galilee	28:16-20	16:15-18				
To more than 500						15:6
To James						15:7
At the Ascension on the Mount of Olives					24:44-49	1:3-8

Matching Chronologically: John 19:16b-19:42. Chronologically arrange the letters of the following descriptions in the order in which they occurred, as well as write the references for the corresponding chapter and verses.

The crucifixion, death, and burial of Jesus: John 19:16b-42

<u>event</u> <u>chapter</u> <u>verses</u>

1. _____, ____ : ____ - ____   A. Jesus gives up his spirit

2. _____, ____ : ____ - ____   B. The crucifixion of Jesus

3. _____, ____ : ____ - ____   C. Jesus gives His mother to the Beloved Disciple

4. _____, ____ : ____ - ____   D. The burial of Jesus

5. _____, ____ : ____ - ____   E. The "notice" on the cross and the Jewish objections

6. _____, ____ : ____ - ____   F. The dividing of Jesus' clothes

7. _____, ____ : ____ - ____   G. The piercing of Jesus' side

The History and Goal of this Discipleship Series

As I began to mature as a Christian, I came to understand the goal of my life should be to obey God for His glorify. God has commanded every believer to make disciples of Jesus Christ throughout the entire world (i.e. Matthew 28:16-20, commonly called the Great Commission). Without a realistic and obtainable plan of action, my goal would be nothing more than a trivialized whimsical wish. So as I began to develop a viable plan to accomplish this monumental task, I quickly became overwhelmed and defeated. How could I possibly reach the world for Christ? For instance, even if I were able to share the gospel with twenty five different people every day for the next thirty years (assuming I live that long), and assuming every person positively responded to the gospel message, I would only reach 0.003 percent of the entire world's population throughout my life. I felt defeated before I even began. I desperately want to obey God by making disciples of all nations, but how am I supposed to accomplish this momentous commission of my Lord?

The Post-Apostolic/Pre-Roman Catholic early church was structured in such a way that encouraged the fulfilling of the Great Commission. Unfortunately, the early church was lacking mature doctrine. It was during the early years of the church that the canon of the New Testament, the hypostatic union of Christ, the trinity, along with many other fundamental doctrines was formulated from the Scriptures. This was no easy task and our early church fathers should be commended. However, by not having maturity in some fundamental doctrines, heresy quickly entered the church and lead to her demise of the proper structure that she obediently possessed in her earlier innocent years. My goal is to reestablish this early church structure in order to provide Christians the opportunity to be obedient in fulfilling the Great Commission while being rooted in sound biblical doctrine. Today, the church (especially in America) has never had greater resources, opportunities, or the freedom to pursue and understand correct doctrine. One of the last pieces of the doctrinal puzzle to be properly understood was eschatology. At the end of the nineteenth century, the church finally began to understand this important doctrine. The theological puzzle is pretty much complete. The church has never had so much correct and proper complete doctrine as she has today. Unfortunately, with the stifling structure that the church inherited from

Session 13

The Resurrection, Appearances, and Ascension of Jesus

<u>event</u>   <u>chapter</u>   <u>verses</u>

Matt.

1. _F_ , _27_ : _62_ - _66_   **A.** Jesus appears, talks, and eats with seven disciples fishing

2. _____ , ___ : ___ - ___   **B.** The Ascension of Jesus

3. _____ , ___ : ___ - ___   **C.** Jesus appears to the disciples the evening of the first day

4. _____ , ___ : ___ - ___   **D.** Mary Magdalene at the tomb

5. _____ , ___ : ___ - ___   **E.** Jesus talks with the two travelers on the road to Emmaus

6. _____ , ___ : ___ - ___   **F.** The tomb is secured/guarded

7. _____ , ___ : ___ - ___   **G.** Jesus appears to Thomas and the other disciples one week later

8. _____ , ___ : ___ - ___   **H.** The guards are paid off to say that Jesus' disciples stole his body

the apostate Roman Catholic Church, this correct complete doctrinal understanding is not easily practiced. My goal is to provide the proper tools and skills so that the church can practice their correct doctrine. With the ability to obtain correct doctrine, combined with a church structure that encourages a biblical reproducible obedient practice, the church could have their greatest opportunity in realizing the fulfillment of the Great Commission.

I plan on making and equipping twelve disciples of Christ by the time I am the age of fifty years old. I will make these disciples by employing a reproducible process so the disciple made can make other disciples. From the age of fifty, I will continue the life-long process of making one disciple every year for the next thirty years of my life. If properly made, these disciples will also make one disciple every year, and then teach them to do the same, and so on. This means I would have personally made a total of forty-two disciples throughout my lifetime; and by doing so, I will have fulfilled the Great Commission. The following is the mathematical potential of this realistic plan of action in fulfilling my goal of obeying Jesus' command commonly called the Great Commission. Again, the key in fulfilling this realistic plan of action is to have a reproducible discipleship method that will not diminish in scope of doctrine or ability for one disciple to make another. God speed as we go forth and make disciples!

1st year .... 12 disciples	16th year .... 393,216 disciples
2nd year .... 24 disciples	17th year .... 786,432 disciples
3rd year .... 48 disciples	18th year .... 1,572,864 disciples
4th year .... 96 disciples	19th year .... 3,145,728 disciples
5th year .... 192 disciples	20th year .... 6,291,456 disciples
6th year .... 384 disciples	21st year .... 12,582,912 disciples
7th year .... 768 disciples	22nd year .... 25,165,824 disciples
8th year .... 1,536 disciples	23rd year .... 50,331,648 disciples
9th year .... 3,072 disciples	24th year .... 100,663,296 disciples
10th year .... 6,144 disciples	25th year .... 201,326,592 disciples
11th year .... 12,288 disciples	26th year .... 402,653,184 disciples
12th year .... 24,576 disciples	27th year .... 805,306,368 disciples
13th year .... 49,152 disciples	28th year ...... 1,610,612,736 disciples
14th year .... 98,304 disciples	29th year ..... 3,221,225,472 disciples
15th year .... 196,608 disciples	30th year ..... 6,442,450,944 disciples

Congratulations!

Now that you have completed the John study, a tool for making disciples who make disciples, what's next? The John discipleship study is the first step in your life-long journey of learning how to get to know God by properly studying the Bible. As you continue to develop this skill through additional progressive discipleship studies, it is also critical for you to help someone else begin their 'getting-to-know-God-through-studying-the-Bible' expedition. These two ingredients (i.e. getting to know God and teaching others how to do the same) are necessary for perpetual spiritual growth. Developing the skills on how to properly interact with the Scriptures will create a positive progressive cycle. This progressive cycle can be referred to as "The John 14:21 Principle." Here is how it works:

- Utilizing a correct biblical hermeneutic will enable the Bible student to exegete (i.e. extrapolate) the Truth of Scripture.

- The Holy Spirit will interact with the Bible student through the Truth of the Bible. It is the Holy Spirit through God's Word that changes and works in people's lives. God's Word is Truth.

- As the Holy Spirit reveals Jesus through the Truth of the Scriptures, one will get to know God (and therefore fall in love with God). To know God is to love God.

- As the disciple of Christ gets to know and therefore love God through the Truth of the Scriptures, they will acquire a natural desire to obey God. Obedience is the key to glorifying, knowing, and growing in Christ.

- As the disciple of Christ gets to know, love, and obey God through the Truth of the Scriptures, they will be loved by Christ (and the Father) and Jesus will show Himself to them (John 14:21). This will now begin the perpetual progressive lifecycle.

The following diagram may help illustrate the John 14:21 principle:

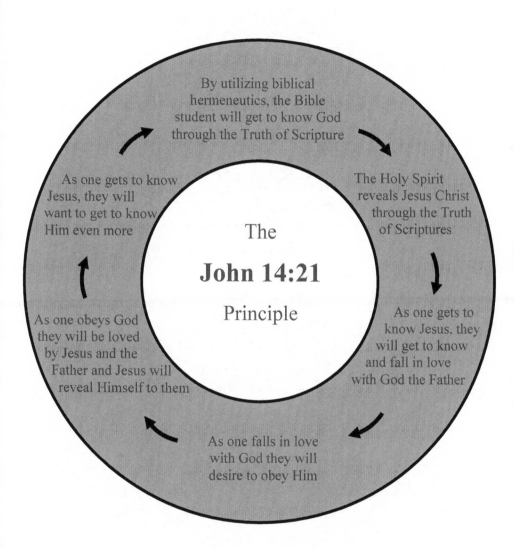

By utilizing biblical hermeneutics, the Bible student will get to know God through the Truth of Scripture

The Holy Spirit reveals Jesus Christ through the Truth of Scriptures

The

John 14:21

Principle

As one gets to know Jesus, they will get to know and fall in love with God the Father

As one falls in love with God they will desire to obey Him

As one obeys God they will be loved by Jesus and the Father and Jesus will reveal Himself to them

As one gets to know Jesus, they will want to get to know Him even more

Conclusion

Jesus has commanded every believer to make disciples. Part of making disciples is teaching them to obey all that Christ has commanded. The John study helps the disciple of Christ accomplish this in the following three ways:

1). Know God through Jesus' commands. Obviously before you can obey Jesus' commands, you need to know what they are. By going through the John study, the student of the Bible will learn how to properly interpret the Scriptures. It is only through correctly interpreting the Scriptures that someone can come to know God by knowing Jesus Christ.

2). Love God by loving others. The love of God will naturally overflow into other's lives as we get to know Him through Jesus Christ. As you grow, you will naturally desire to see others come to know the Father through Jesus. You can begin their journey of knowing God through the reproducible John study. And then you can help them do the same.

3). Obey Jesus' commands. While the student of the Bible is learning the commands of Christ, they are also being renewed and transformed into Jesus Christ by the Holy Spirit through the Truth of Scripture. The student of the Bible will become increasingly motivated to obey Jesus as their love for God continually grows as they get to know Him through Christ.

So one of the next steps upon completing the John discipleship study is to find someone you can take through the John discipleship study. Ask the person who took you through this John study to help you take someone else through this study.

The John discipler's edition has been designed to help people take others through the John study. The following are some of the practical aspects of the John discipler's edition:

- The page numbers of the discipler's edition workbook match the page numbers of the future disciple's workbook. Therefore, the pages of both John study workbooks correspond.

- Everything in the future disciple's workbook is seen as a light grey within the discipler's edition workbook. Anything appearing in a black font is only contained within the discipler's edition workbook.

- Every session has the answers to every question. However, it is important to remember that 'getting the correct answer' is not the desired emphasis. The purpose of the questions is to help in making a disciple of Jesus Christ.

- Every question (when applicable) has the reference (i.e. book, chapter, and verse) to every question.

- Every session has additional information to help the discipler. The discipler will find the additional information and commentary are mostly located on pages in their workbook that correspond to the blank pages labeled as "notes" within the future disciple's workbook. This information is given to help the discipler better understand the purpose of the questions within the John study.

- At the beginning of the additional information and commentary section of each session there is a short paragraph entitled, "Keep the Focus." This information is to remind the discipler of various valuable discipleship principles. The John study is not simply another 'Bible study.' The John study is designed to be a reproducible discipleship tool.

Conclusion

- Finally, there is a DVD to help equip the discipler to effectively take a future disciple through each session of the John study. This DVD shares various experiences and insights that other disciplers have had in utilizing the John study in making disciples.

Along with taking someone through the John discipleship study, you should also personally continue to develop your skills in learning how to study the Bible. There are several other reproducible studies that you and your discipler can discuss and decide what would be best.

Made in the USA
Charleston, SC
27 May 2015

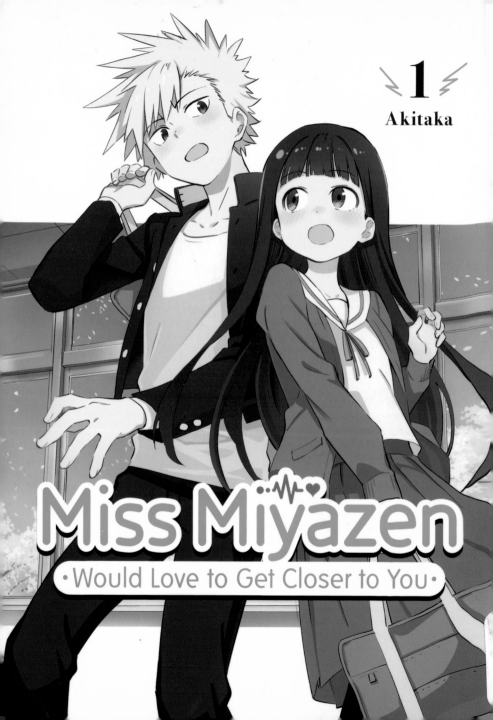

Miss Miyazen
•Would Love to Get Closer to You•

1

Akitaka

I'd love to be friends!

Two high school classmates, Sakura Miyazen and Sota Matsubayashi, are polar opposites: Miyazen is a prim and proper young lady, while Matsubayashi is a brusque former troublemaker. They're secretly dying to talk to each other, but their backgrounds are so different, they can't seem to strike up a conversation! And why does a simple greeting make the both of them turn red?!

A cute and light-hearted romantic comedy that will have you rooting for the pair to get closer!

Logo design by Abigail Blackman

Printed in the U.S.A.
www.kodansha.us

RATED:
13+

USA
$12.95

CAN
$17.50

ISBN 978-1-64729-141-9

51295>

9 781647 291419

EAN

KODANSHA

AFTERWORD

Thank you for reading this far. I'm Akitaka.
Most of my works until now have been on the longer side,
so I was nervous drawing such short chapters.
But once I got started, I managed somehow to do all right,
and the next thing I knew, I had a whole book.
I hope I can continue to bring you more of
this story as the pair gets closer.

SPECIAL THANKS

Yuki Tabei   Editor Y-moto
Hiroki Misaki
Daimaru   All of my dear
                  readers

Miss Miyazen Would
Love to Get Closer to You 1

A VERTICAL Book

Editor: Michelle Lin
Translation: Jenny McKeon
Production: Grace Lu
Pei Ann Yeap
Mercedes McGarry
Proofreading: Micah Q. Allen

Originally published in Japanese as *Ochikaduki ni Naritai Miyazen-san 1* by
SQUARE ENIX CO., LTD., 2020
Ochikaduki ni Naritai Miyazen-san first serialized in *Gekkan Gangan Joker*,
SQUARE ENIX CO., LTD., 2020-2021

This is a work of fiction.

ISBN: 978-1-64729-141-9

Printed in the United States of America

First Edition

Kodansha USA Publishing, LLC
451 Park Avenue South
7th Floor
New York, NY 10016
www.kodansha.us

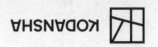
KODANSHA

THANK YOU VERY MUCH.

Y-YOU DROPPED THIS.

I CAN GO ON FOREVER ABOUT MY FAVORITE MANGA AND MOVIES AND STUFF, BUT...

BUT I'M SO AWKWARD, I'D PROBABLY ONLY BE ABLE TO TALK ABOUT OUR COMMON INTERESTS.

PLUNK

I'LL PAY YOU BACK... IN HELL.

NO, WAIT. WASN'T THAT...

HER SMILE'S CU—

HUH?

SMILE

DON'T TELL ME WE LIKE THE SAME KINDA STUFF ...?

A LINE FROM THE MOVIE *YAKUZA LANGUAGE*?

I'LL PAY YOU BACK...IN HELL.

THERE'S NO WAY SHE WATCHES GORY MOVIES LIKE THAT.

TEE HEE

SHE'D PROBABLY FAINT IF SHE SAW A BUG KICK THE BUCKET.

NO.

GOOD...

I'M JUST HEARING THINGS 'CAUSE I DIDN'T GET ENOUGH SLEEP.

SLUMP

... HEAVENS, THAT DIDN'T GET THROUGH TO HIM AT ALLLL!

WHY? HE WAS SUPPOSED TO SAY, "YOU LIKE THAT STUFF, TOO, MIYAZEN?"

I WOULD LOVE TO GET CLOSER TO MATSUBAYASHI, SO I WENT AND STUDIED UP ON HIS INTERESTS...

AAAAAAAH

BUT IF THE REFERENCE WASN'T CLEAR, I MUST'VE JUST SEEMED LIKE A TOTAL WEIRDO!

WE'RE IN THE MIDDLE OF CLASS, YOU TWO.

WHAT AM I GONNA DO...?

AAAH... WHAT DO I DO NOW?

Chapter 1
A Pair Who Would Love
to Get Closer

SPRING, THE FIRST DAY OF SCHOOL.

MY NAME IS SAKURA MIYAZEN.

I WENT TO OKAZAKA ACADEMY. PLEASED TO MEET YOU ALL.

SO DO YOU HAVE, LIKE, A BUTLER?

MY FAMILY DECIDED TO MOVE HERE.

WOW!

ISN'T OKAZAKA THAT FARAWAY SCHOOL FOR RICH GIRLS?

8

NOW ME, ON THE OTHER HAND...

UH, I'M SOTA MATSU-BAYASHI.

WENT TO GINBUSHI JUNIOR HIGH.

...NICE TO MEET YA.

GLOWER

DID HE BRIBE SOMEONE...?

HOW DID HE GET INTO OUR SCHOOL ...?

MAYBE HE THREATENED THE PRINCIPAL...

THAT PLACE'S FAMOUS FOR ITS DELINQUENTS...!!

NERVOUS

ど
ど

NERVOUS

GINBUSHI JUNIOR HIGH...?!

しん...
SILENCE...

OH, COME OOOOOOON !!

I WAS SET IN STONE AS A WOLF AMONG SHEEP.

I HAD AN OLD PAL TUTOR ME LIKE CRAZY, AND I STUDIED HARD FOR THE ENTRANCE EXAMS, OKAY?!

URK!

No sleeping.

I HAVEN'T EVEN DONE ANYTHING! AND I'M ON THE STRAIGHT AND NARROW THESE DAYS!

...WAIT. IS THAT WHY PEOPLE AVOID ME?

RATTLE

SURE, I MIGHT STILL HAVE SOME BAD HABITS AND ATTITUDES, BUT...

UM,

OH WELL, BEING LEFT ALONE ISN'T SO BAD, EITHER. I CAN ENJOY SOME PEACE AND QUIET...

IT'S A PLEASURE TO MEET YOU,

MATSU-BAYASHI.

SHE'S GREETED ME...

GOOD MORNING.

YO.

SINCE THEN,

GOOD MORNING, MATSU-BAYASHI.

EVERY DAY WITHOUT FAIL.

Good morni

Good mor

Yo.

Yo.

I COULDN'T FIGURE IT OUT IN THE END.

AND THERE WAS ALSO THIS...

I'LL PAY YOU BACK...IN HELL.

I'M SURE MIYAZEN SAYS HI TO EVERYONE.

NO ONE ELSE TALKS TO ME, THOUGH, SO I'M SERIOUSLY GRATEFUL.

Good morning!

BUT IT MAKES ME REALLY HAPPY...!!

I WANNA AT LEAST GIVE HER A FRIENDLIER RESPONSE THAN A GRUNT...

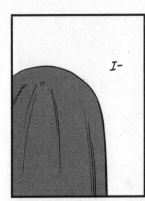

I-

I TRY MY BEST AND GREET HIM EVERY DAY, BUT IT NEVER GOES FURTHER THAN THAT...

I DON'T THINK WE'RE GETTING ANY CLOSER TODAY, EITHER...!

DO I GET NERVOUS AROUND MATSU-BAYASHI ...?

I CAN CONVERSE WITH OTHER PEOPLE JUST FINE, THOUGH.

IS IT BECAUSE I QUOTED THAT MOVIE THE OTHER DAY? BUT IT DIDN'T GET THROUGH TO HIM!...

COULD IT BE THAT HE ACTUALLY HATES ME...?!

AND HE DOESN'T REALLY SEEM INTERESTED IN TALKING TO ME.

THE MORE I THINK ABOUT IT, THE MORE MUDDLED IT MAKES ME!

AHH!

I WISH I COULD GET TO KNOW HIM AND CHAT WITH HIM AND SO ON.

WE SIT SO CLOSE TO EACH OTHER.

SIGH
はぁ

17

THEN I'M SURE WE'D BE ABLE TO GET CLOSER...

JOLT

GLANCE

OH MY.

O- UM.

AAAAAH! THAT WAS SUCH AN AWKWARD COVER-UP...!

?!

WHAT IS THIS TRASH DOING HERE...?

WH-

YEAH, MAYBE.

AM I REALLY THAT SCARY...?

HRMM...

GUESS...IT TAKES SOME COURAGE TO TALK TO A FACE LIKE THIS.

NOW THAT THE ENVIRONMENT'S DIFFERENT, IT'S PRETTY TOUGH...

COME TO THINK OF IT, PEOPLE SAID THE SAME THING TO ME IN JUNIOR HIGH.

AT THE TIME, IT HELPED KEEP THE WEIRDOS AWAY, BUT...

OH.

YEAH.

UH,

G-

GOODBYE,

MATSU-
BAYASHI.

W-WELL, IF YOU'LL EXCUSE ME.

I DON'T GET THIS FREAKED OUT WHEN I TALK TO OTHER GIRLS.

WHAT AM I, A CHICKEN...?

DAMMIT... I GAVE HER ANOTHER HALF-ASSED RESPONSE...

"IT'S A PLEASURE TO MEET YOU,

MATSU-BAYASHI."

GUESS IT TAKES SOME COURAGE TO TALK TO A FACE LIKE THIS...

AND MAYBE HE REALLY DOES HATE ME...

I KNEW IT. I'M A BIRD-BRAIN, AREN'T I...?

AAAH... I CAN'T DO IT!

MIYA-ZEN!

...?

I-IS SOMETHING THE MATTER ...?

24

WHEW. GUESS THAT WAS BETTER THAN NOTHING ...

U-

BYE ...

UM...!

26

WHA?!

ERM...

I'M NOT SURE HOW TO TELL YOU THIS, BUT...

BUT WHAT THE HELL'S GOING ON?!

SHE'S SO CLOSE...! THIS IS THE CLOSEST SHE'S EVER BEEN...!

FOR REAL...?!

NO WAY...

I'M AFRAID WE DON'T HAVE SCHOOL TOMORROW...

NO, I CAN'T JUST LEAVE LIKE THIS.

BUT I WANNA CRAWL INTO A HOLE AND NEVER COME OUT!

I-I WANNA GET OUTTA HERE!

BOMF

OH, NO, S'FINE...

AH, I'M SORRY. I DIDN'T MEAN TO BE RUDE!

FWIP

SO, UM...

IT'S A WEEK-END,

IF ONLY A TRAPDOOR WOULD MAGI-CALLY APPEAR AND OPEN UP BELOW ME...

PLEASE JUST LET ME DIE!...

29

YEAH.

SEE YA THEN.

I-I'M SO SORRY...

TOOK YA LONG ENOUGH, MIYAZEN.

WH-WHAT IS IT...?

HMMM?

HM?

DID SOMETHING GOOD HAPPEN?

HUH?

NO, THANK YOU VERY MUCH!

N-

WANT ME TO GUESS WHO IT WAS?

H-HOW CAN YOU TELL...?

SOMETHING GOOD HAPPEN?

...

HEY, SORRY, I'M LATE.

YOU SURE ARE, DUDE.

"HELL YEAH"?!

HELL YEAH...

MONDAY.

YOU KNOW I CAN'T DO THAT.

YUP.

ONLY IF YOU BEAT ME AT ARM WRESTLING.

WHAT? C'MON, TELL ME.

MATSU-
BAYASHI,

THEY
GOT JUST A
LITTLE BIT
CLOSER.

MORN-
ING,

MIYA-
ZEN.

GOOD
MORNING!

AND EVEN THAT'S KINDA AWKWARD.

...BUT SO FAR, WE'VE JUST BEEN GREETING EACH OTHER.

I WANNA HAVE FUN CHATTING WITH MIYAZEN.

Chapter 2 Shootin'

LOVELY WEATHER, ISN'T IT, MATSU-BAYASHI?

Good morning.

NOT LIKE I GET MANY CHANCES TO TALK TO HER, ANYWAY...

O-O-O-OKAY, CALM DOWN! WH-WHAT DO I SAY?

Uh... Uh-huh...

HUH?! IS THIS A CHANCE?

THE PERFECT WEATHER FOR A SHOOTIN'.

I-ISN'T THAT A LINE...

HUH?

THEN WE CAN TOTALLY CHAT! MY INTERESTS ARE THE ONE THING I HAVE NO PROBLEM TALKING ABOUT...!

MAYBE SHE LIKES THE SAME STUFF AS ME, AFTER ALL!

SHOOTIN'

FROM YAKUZA ELEVEN, ONE OF MY FAVORITE MOVIES?

PERFECT WEATHER FOR A SHOOTIN'.

I'VE WATCHED THAT MOVIE SO MANY TIMES, I ALMOST GOT THE WRONG IDEA.

GRAMS TOLD ME ABOUT A KIDS' GAME LIKE THAT FROM BACK IN THE DAY.

MAYBE SHE MEANS SHOOTIN' MARBLES...!

NO, WAIT A SEC...

OLD SCHOOL?

TH-THAT'S COOL. VERY OLD SCHOOL.

Shootin' marbles.

N-NO, I MEAN... YOU KNOW, LIKE THIS...

KAPOW KAPOW

OH, IS THAT HOW YOU PLAY WITH THEM?

?!!

ACK!

DID HE UNDERSTAND ME WRONG AGAIN...?

HMMM? "SHOOTIN'" IS THE RIGHT WORD, RIGHT? HMM?

THEY GOT JUST AN EIGHTH OF AN INCH CLOSER.

THAT CONVERSATION WENT PRETTY WELL, YEAH...?!

I DID IT...!

Hmm?

I WAS HOPING WE'D FINALLY BE ABLE TO TALK ABOUT MOVIES...

Miss Miyazen
Would Love to
Get Closer to You

HUH. MIYAZEN USUALLY BRINGS A BENTO, BUT SHE'S BUYING LUNCH TODAY.

Chapter 3 Responsibility

MMMGH...

NO, WAIT! I SHOULDN'T BOTHER HER IF SHE'S EATING WITH A PAL...

I WANNA TALK TO HER.

BONK

OH, MATSUBA-

UH, UM...

N-NAH, IT'S FINE. I WAS SPACIN' OUT...

AH, I'M SO SORRY! I GOT WATER ON YOU ...!

SHE'S HOLDING OUT HER PINKY!

DO...

JUST LIKE WHEN THEY CUT 'EM OFF IN THE MOVIES I WATCH!

I'LL TAKE RESPONSIBILITY FOR IT.

THIS HAS TO MEAN MIYAZEN LIKES YAKUZA MOVIES, TOO, RIGHT?

DO I PERHAPS NEED TO...TAKE RESPONSIBILITY...?

TO MOST PEOPLE, A PINKY MEANS...!

ZWOOSH

A PRINCESS LIKE MIYAZEN WOULD NEVER MAKE A YAKUZA REFERENCE...!

NO. THINK IT THROUGH, IDIOT...!

TUG

JUST DON'T DO IT AGAIN, YEAH?

IT'S A PROMISE.

BUT THIS ISN'T SO BAD, EITHER...!

OKAY~

TH-THAT'S NOT WHAT I MEAN...!

HE WAS SUPPOSED TO SAY, "I DIDN'T EXPECT YOU TO MAKE THAT REFERENCE, MIYAZEN!" AND THEN I WOULD'VE ASKED IF HE WANTED TO EAT LUNCH TOGETHER...!

M-MY PINKY TOUCHED HERRRS!

HIS RAMEN GOT SOGGY.

Her omelet rice got cold.

Miss Miyazen
Would Love to
Get Closer to You

JUST ME AND HER...!

I'VE GOT CLASS DUTIES WITH MIYAZEN TODAY.

Chapter 4 Cat

POMF
POMF
POMF
POMF

....

....

OH, SURE!

MIYAZEN, CAN YOU DO THAT ONE?

MYOOOW♪

KYOOOT!

CUTE

UH...

AH!

WHIP

AH!

FWIP

CATS SURE ARE CUTE, HUH?

I'M BEING WAY TOO SELF-CONSCIOUS!

FOR A MOMENT, I THOUGHT HE MEANT ME!

Y-YES!

YEAH, S'COOL HOW CHILL THEY ARE.

C-CATS ARE SO CALMING TO WATCH, AREN'T THEY?

WHOA, I SAID IT OUT LOUD!

THEY MANAGED TO GET A LITTLE CLOSER.

IT WAS EMBAR-RASSING, BUT I'M GLAD WE GOT TO TALK...

BADUMP

BADUMP

Miss Miyazen
Would Love to
Get Closer to You

SHIV!

SHIV

DID I HEAR WRONG? OR IS IT A WORD IN THE KYOTO DIALECT?

YEAH, RIGHT! EVEN THOSE GUYS DON'T GREET EACH OTHER LIKE THAT!

THAT GREETING... IT'S FROM ONE OF MY YAKUZA MOVIES...

SHIV!

—Nope.

SHIV ?!

SHE'S FREAKIN' OUT ABOUT SOMETHING...

I'M FINE, THANK YOU...

I-

OH.

HUH ?

YOU OKAY, MIYAZEN ...?

BUT...

IT MUST BE BECAUSE OF THE MOVIE I WATCHED LAST NIGHT...

←SHIV

HMMM?! I-I GOT SO THROWN OFF, I BLURTED OUT SOMETHING STRANGE!!

THAT WAS THE FIRST TIME MATSU-BAYASHI'S GREETED ME FIRST...

HOW COULD I NOT GET FLUSTERED ...?

"SHIVAZEN"... HE'S GOING TO START CALLING ME "SHIVAZEN"!

AAH, BUT I CAN'T BELIEVE I SAID "SHIV"...

"SHIVAZEN" WAS THE FURTHEST THING FROM MATSU-BAYASHI'S MIND.

I CAN'T BELIEVE I SAID HI TO HER FIRST...!

THUMP THUMP

Shiv~

— Wrong.

Miss Miyazen
Would Love to
Get Closer to You

Chapter 6 Friends

GOOD MORN-ING,

MATSU-BAYASHI.

OH, YEAH? THANKS.

I BELIEVE OUR CLASS WILL BE IN THE SCIENCE LAB TODAY.

HEYA.

See ya.

I WANNA KEEP GETTING TO KNOW HER BETTER, BUT...

I CAN FINALLY TALK TO MIYAZEN A LITTLE, EVEN IF IT'S JUST BASIC STUFF.

YUP, THERE IT IS.

GOSH, YOU'RE SO BRAVE!

YOU CHAT WITH MATSU-BAYASHI LIKE IT'S NO BIG DEAL.

THAT'S AMAZING, MIYAZEN!

REALLY? I THINK HE'S PRETTY APPROACH-ABLE...

I CAN HEAR YOU, Y'KNOW ...?

I'D FREAK OUT IF I WERE YOU. HE'S WAY TOO SCARY.

BUT I DON'T REALLY WANT ANYONE SAYING STUFF TO MIYAZEN 'CAUSE OF ME...

I GOT USED TO PEOPLE BADMOUTHING ME IN JUNIOR HIGH,

Oh, I watched it!

By the way, that TV show last night...

Hrmmm.

WHAT DO YOU MEAN?

"ALL RIGHT" ...?

REALLY, THOUGH. ARE YOU GONNA BE ALL RIGHT?

UM, I'M PRETTY SURE IT'S SOME KINDA METAPHOR...

H-HE DESTROYED A MOUNTAIN? AMAZING...!

I HEARD MATSU-BAYASHI WAS A REAL TROUBLE-MAKER IN HIS JUNIOR HIGH SCHOOL.

SO YOU MIGHT WANNA BE CAREFUL.

SOME PEOPLE ARE GONNA SPREAD WEIRD RUMORS THAT YOU'RE CONNECTED WITH GUYS LIKE HIM,

THEY EVEN CALLED HIM "MOUNTAIN-BREAKER MATSUBA-YASHI," YOU KNOW?

THAT'D BE BAD...!

SO IT'D BOTHER YOU?

HUH?

CONNECTED
=
TOGETHER
=
DATING

SHE'S THE TYPE TO CARE ABOUT WHAT SOCIETY THINKS OF HER...?

HIGH SCHOOL IS SCARY...

COULD EXCHANGING A FEW WORDS REALLY IMPLY THAT WE'RE DATING?

I-I WONDER IF SHE GETS IT NOW...

WELL, THAT WAS QUITE EDUCATIONAL. THANK YOU VERY MUCH!

WE JUST NEED TO BECOME CLOSE FRIENDS! THEN NO ONE WILL ASSUME WE'RE DATING!

I'VE GOT TO TRY HARDER...

DOESN'T GET IT.

WANNA HIT THE CAFETERIA WITH ME TODAY?

SURE, I'LL GO FIND YA AT NOON.

WHAT SHOULD I DO NEXT...?

BUT SO FAR, I'VE ONLY MANAGED TO HAVE BRIEF CONVERSATIONS WITH HIM...

LUNCH-TIME.

THE CLASSROOM'S TOO NOISY, AND I CAN'T AFFORD TO BUY SCHOOL LUNCH EVERY DAY.

NO ONE COMES HERE, BUT THIS IS THE BEST SEAT IN THE HOUSE.

UM...

GOTTA SAY, I KILLED THESE MINCEMEAT RICE BALLS. SEASONING'S JUST RIGHT.

MHM.

POP

WOULD YOU MIND IF I JOINED YOU?

O-OH... YEAH...?

I WANTED TO TRY EATING SOME- WHERE HIGH UP...

WHAT'RE YOU DOING HERE?

M-M-M-MIYAZEN?!

A-

SHE'S TOTALLY GOT FRIENDS IN CLASS, UNLIKE ME...

I MEAN, I'M SUPER PUMPED, BUT WHY?!

CRUMBLE CRUMBLE

SO I THOUGHT THIS WOULD BE THE PERFECT WAY FOR US TO BECOME BETTER FRIENDS.

THEY SAY BREAKING BREAD TOGETHER BRINGS PEOPLE CLOSER,

AM I BEING TOO BOLD?!

BUT DOESN'T EATING LUNCH ALONE TOGETHER LOOK MORE LIKE WE'RE DATING...?!

I KNEW IT! THEY'D THINK WE'RE TOGETHER!

PEOPLE MIGHT GET THE WRONG IDEA IF YOU HANG AROUND A GUY LIKE ME.

...YOU SURE ABOUT THIS?

D-DON'T WORRY. IF IT COMES DOWN TO IT, I'LL BE SURE TO EXPLAIN...!

BUT IF I JUST SAY THAT WE'RE FRIENDS, IT SHOULD BE FINE...!

SO THIS REALLY MIGHT GIVE SOMEONE THE IMPRESSION THAT WE'RE DATING...

HAAH.

UH... COOL.

WAIT, SO IF SOMEONE SHOWS UP, SHE'S GONNA SAY SHE DOESN'T KNOW ME...?

PRETTY RELAT- ABLE FOR A PRINCESS.

WOW, SO SHE BUYS RICE BALLS FROM CONVENIENCE STORES, TOO?

BUT WHAT IN THE WORLD IS THIS PACKAGING...?

MATSU-BAYASHI ALWAYS EATS RICE BALLS, SO I THOUGHT I'D DO THE SAME,

I'LL HELP YOU.

TH-

THANK YOU VERY MUCH.

HERE.

PEEL

PEEL

71

MATSU-BAYASHI, ARE YOURS HOMEMADE, BY ANY CHANCE?

Delicious!

OH, YEAH... I'M THE ONLY ONE WHO COOKS AT HOME.

AH, THERE'S A TRICK TO THAT.

I CAN'T EVEN GET A RICE BALL TO COME OUT RIGHT...

YOU MAKE YOUR OWN BENTO? THAT'S AMAZING!

It gets too dry...

WOULD YOU MIND IF I JOINED YOU?

I WAS GONNA SAY NO, SINCE I DON'T WANNA CAUSE HER TROUBLE...

THE TRUTH IS...

BUT I COULDN'T BRING MYSELF TO DO IT.

WE COULD
STAY HERE
LIKE THIS
FOREVER.

IF ONLY

HIDE
?

WHY
...?

MIYAZEN,
DO ME
A FAVOR
AND HIDE.

IT'S
PROBA-
BLY A
TEACHER.

TMP

TMP

TMP

OH.

THAT CAN'T...

TH-

YOU MIGHT GET WRITTEN UP OR SOMETHIN' IF THEY FIND YOU TOGETHER WITH ME.

Together ...!

YOU FOUND A GREAT SPOT.

NICE AND QUIET, RIGHT?

HM? WHAT'S UP? LET ME THROUGH.

IT'S YOU, MATSU-BAYASHI?

H-HEY...

A TYPHOON?

IT'S, LIKE, 50 MILES AN HOUR, SO...

TH-THE WIND'S REAL STRONG OUT HERE.

O-OF COURSE NOT, SIR.

DON'T TELL ME YOU'RE UP TO SOMETHING SKETCHY?

OKAY, YOU'RE BEING SUPER WEIRD.

I-I'LL DO IT FOR YA.

C'MON, I'M SUPPOSED TO INSPECT THE ROOF.

OOF, YOU'RE REALLY STRONG.

FINE, THEN I'LL JUST FORCE MY WAY THROUGH...

OH MY~

O-

URGG

URGG

URGG

HE'S COVERING FOR ME SO THAT TEACHER DOESN'T GET THE WRONG IDEA AND THINK WE'RE TOGETHER...?

THAT WAS SO FORCED...

IT'S PERFECTLY SAFE NOW, SIR~

IT LOOKS LIKE THE WIND JUST DIED DOWN.

You were alone up here...

DON'T TELL ME...

YOU TWO...

AH!

YES!

NO, SHE HAPPENED TO...

77

WE WERE JUST HANGING OUT AS FRIENDS...!

THANK YOU FOR UNDER-STANDING...!

WELL, MAKE SURE YOU'RE NOT LATE FOR CLASS.

A-AHH... FRIENDS, HUH?

OH.

BUT IT LOOKS LIKE HE'S GETTING ALONG JUST FINE.

I WAS WORRIED IF MATSUBAYASHI WAS FITTING IN,

I SHOULD APOLOGIZE, TOO...FOR SPEAKING OUT OF TURN.

NO,

YEAH, THAT DID KINDA TURN INTO A WHOLE THING...

GOOD-NESS, WHAT A FRIGHT~

SORRY.

A-

"FRIENDS."

OF COURSE!

TOGETH-?!

BUT HE DIDN'T GET THE WRONG IDEA AND THINK WE'RE TOGETHER...!

H-HMM....?!

THEY PROBABLY JUST MEANT, LIKE, SOCIALLY...

I-I WAS TOLD PEOPLE MIGHT THINK I'M CONNECTED TO YOU...

W-WAS SOMEONE SPREADING RUMORS LIKE THAT...?

HUH?

I WAS THE ONE GETTING THE WRONG IDEA THIS WHOLE TIME?!

MIYA-ZEN?

SHE MISUN-DERSTOOD, BUT THEY STILL GOT SOMEWHAT CLOSER.

Hmmm?

Miss Miyazen
Would Love to
Get Closer to You

AND THEN, IF THINGS GO WELL, WE CAN HAVE FUN CHATTING ABOUT IT!

I WANNA RECOMMEND A YAKUZA MOVIE TO MIYAZEN.

Chapter 7 Mixed Up

IF I SAY STUFF LIKE THAT, I'LL JUST SEEM EVEN SCARIER...

DO YA LIKE... YAKUZA MOVIES?

OH! BUT...!

M-MIYAZEN.

MAYBE I SHOULD SET THE BAR A LITTLE LOWER...

DO YA LIKE SCARY MOVIES ...?

YAKUZA HOUSE CALL DVD

SCARY ONES ...?

...?

COME TO THINK OF IT, I THOUGHT MATSUBAYASHI WAS A BIT FRIGHTENING AT FIRST, TOO.

POP

AND THERE ARE STILL SOME THINGS I CAN'T HANDLE VERY WELL...

I WAS A LITTLE FRIGHTENED IN THE BEGINNING...

NERVOUS

WHATCHA LOOKIN' AT, FRESH MEAT?!

NERVOUS

...BUT I GRADUALLY STARTED TO NOTICE THE GOOD PARTS...

I'LL HANDLE THIS. GET OUTTA HERE!

AND NOW IT'S ALMOST LIKE I CAN'T LOOK AWAY...

I'LL TAKE RESPONSIBI~ FOR WHAT HAPPENED.

I THINK I'M GETTING QUITE FOND OF...

THE WAY MY HEART POUNDS WHEN I WATCH...

THEN MAYBE SHE'LL EVEN TRY YAKUZA MOVIES SOMEDAY ...!

SO SHE'S UP FOR WATCHING SCARY STUFF.

C-COOL.

H-HMM ...?

• • •

HMMM?!

DID I GET MIXED UP AND START TALKING ABOUT MATSUBAYASHI PARTWAY THROUGH?

MIYAZEN WAS JUST BEGINNING TO GET HOOKED ON BOTH.

Miss Miyazen
Would Love to
Get Closer to You

I'll help if you want to catch that guy...

— Watching a film in the multimedia room.

I WISH THEY'D JUST SHOW US A YAKUZA ONE INSTEAD.

MMM. THIS MOVIE'S GOT SOME DRAMA AND DRIVE, BUT IT'S NOT MY THING...

BANG
POW
POW
POW
BANG

There he is! Get him!

BUT I WONDER IF SHE CAN HANDLE STUFF LIKE THIS?

...MIYAZEN SAID SCARY MOVIES FREAK HER OUT,

AH.

AAAGH!

PANG
PANG

SQUEEEZE

NO WAY SHE COULD DO MY YAKUZA MOVIES, THEN.

MAYBE IT'S THE BLOOD AND GORE SHE CAN'T STAND?

— She watches them.

CLICK BOOM

BOOM

PEEEEK... ...

QUIET DOWN, YOU TWO.

AH... NO, I JUST, ERM...!

YOU DON'T NEED TO FORCE YOUR-SELF, MIYAZEN.

NOW I'VE GONE AND DONE IT!

MATSU-BAYASHI MUST'VE REALIZED I CAN'T HANDLE FRIGHTENING SCENES.

I'VE PRACTICED SO MUCH, BUT THEY'RE STILL TOO SCARY FOR ME...

TO BE ABLE TO WATCH THE THINGS HE LIKES.

BUT I WANT...

MATSU-BAYASHI...

AND THEN, MAYBE SOME-DAY...

I'LL DO MY BEST, I PROMISE.

CON-CEN-TRATE, WILL YA?

AND SHE WHISPERED IN MY EEEEEAR!

SHE'S SO STUDIOUS. I'M BARELY EVEN PAYING ATTENTION...

O-OH...

BOOM PA PA PA PA KABOOM POW

EEEEEEK!

BADUMP BADUMP

Miss Miyazen
Would Love to
Get Closer to You

HAAH

HAAH

HUFF

WHEEZE

ぜ"

WHEEZE

ぜ"

Chapter 9 Marathon

DID IT COME TO THIS...?!

WH-WHY...

I THOUGHT A MARATHON WOULD GIVE ME A CHANCE TO TALK TO MATSU-BAYASHI!...!

NEVER MIND "GETTING CLOSER," HE'S GETTING FARTHER AND FARTHER AWAY...!

(P.E. Grade: A)

ZOOM

AAAAH!

IT MUST BE MY PUNISHMENT FOR NOT TAKING EXERCISE SERIOUSLY!

AAH, THE SIDE OF MY STOMACH HURTS...

The night air's nice and cool~

I'VE BEEN JOGGING TO GET IN SHAPE FOR TODAY, BUT THIS IS ON ANOTHER LEVEL...

YOU OKAY, MIYAZEN ...?

Y-

WHEEZE

WHEEZE

SHE WAS CLOSE BEHIND ME AND THEN JUST DISAPPEARED...

SHE MUSTA PUSHED HERSELF TOO HARD AND CRASHED.

AH, SHE'LL FIGURE OUT I SPED UP 'CAUSE I WAS WORRIED ABOUT HER!

BUT WHY DID YOU FINISH YOUR FIRST LAP SO QUICKLY...?

I'M ON MY SECOND LAP.

M-MATSUBAYASHI? WHY'RE YOU...?

WOW!

I-I WAS HAVING SO MUCH FUN RUNNING ...

I DIDN'T NOTICE.

STILL, I'M SO HAPPY!

THANK YOU VERY MUCH, MATSUBA-YASHI!

HUH? NO, LIKE I SAID, I JUST...

YES, BUT...!

THEY GOT CLOSER IN THE END.

Miss Miyazen
Would Love to
Get Closer to You

THAT BUMP... WHAT HAPPENED?!

A-ARE YOU OKAY?

OH, YOU'RE RIGHT. IT'S SWOLLEN.

HUH?

THERE'S THIS VIOLENT PERSON...

I JUST GOT IN A BIG FIGHT BEFORE SCHOOL.

YEAH, I'M FINE.

VIOLENT...

A BIG FIGHT...

A FEARSOME BEAST...

IF I FIGHT BACK, THE CLAWS COME RIGHT OUT.

UNAVOID-ABLE...

WHO'S ALWAYS COMPLAINING, GETTING ON MY CASE.

I CAN'T TURN A BLIND EYE IF MATSU-BAYASHI'S IN DAN-GER...!

UM...!

SO A LITTLE BUMP LIKE THIS IS NOTHING NEW...

DMP

DMP...

DOES HE FIGHT THAT BEAST ALL THE TIME...?

I'LL COME WITH YOU TO TALK TO THEM, SO...!

Y-YOU SHOULD ASK THEM TO STOP!

NO, WAIT!

KA-BAM

HER HANDS ARE SO SMALL...

KER-POW

KA-THUD

(It's his heart pounding.)

AH.

HM...?

WHY'S SHE SO WORKED UP ALL OF A SUDDEN? IT'S NOT LIKE HER...

SQUEEEEZE

But you went back to sleep.

スコーン

PLONK

I told ya to wake me up!

IT'S, LIKE, A FAMILY FIGHT...

UH... THING IS,

I'M SO SORRY...

I- U

NAH...

CLENCH...

MATSU- BAYASHI WAS NOTHING BUT GRATEFUL.

I'LL COM WITH YOU TAL TO YOU FAM

Miyazen stuck it on for him.

Miss Miyazen
Would Love to
Get Closer to You

YEAH.

THIS LITTLE ONE'S GOTTEN QUITE FRIENDLY.

Bonus Story
Chapter 11 Cats and Dogs

HEH HEH

SO YOU REMEMBER US NOW, BUDDY?

MYAAAH

ARE YOU A CAT PERSON, MATSU-BAYASHI?

I LIKE COOL DOGS.

I GUESS I'M MORE OF A DOG GUY.

COOL (INTENSE EYES)

BUT THIS LITTLE KITTY IS JUST SO CUTE...!

I KNOW, RIGHT? I'M A DOG PERSON AS WELL.

BUT I MIGHT HAFTA SWITCH SIDES IF I KEEP PETTING THIS ONE...

HUH?

BLOND →

BIG →

DEPENDABLE →

GENTLE →

YEAH.

WHAT?

I-I'M TALKING ABOUT MY GOLDEN RETRIEVER!

MY BAD. I'VE BEEN DOING ALL THE PETTING.

OH,

...

YES, THEY MIGHT BE SIMILAR IN SOME WAYS, BUT...!

WHAT IN THE WORLD WAS I COMPARING JUST NOW...?

WHAAAA?!

THERE, GO OVER TO MIYAZEN.

I-I THINK I'M SEEING THINGS...

RUB

MYOWWW

OH, YOU! THIS CUTENESS JUST ISN'T FAIR!

PURR PURR

MEOW~

POOF

MYOWW

MYA~

POOF

MYOWW?

MOW...

MYAAAH

MATSU-BAYASHI!

IS IT 'CAUSE WE WERE TALKING ABOUT ANIMALS...?

HUH...? AM I EXHAUSTED OR WHAT...?

Chapter 12 Broad

...IS THAT GUY A FRIEND OF HERS?

IT'S MIYA-ZEN.

U-UM... I DON'T THINK...

C'MON, LET'S JUST GRAB A DRINK.

...? MY CHEST FEELS FUNNY. WHAT'S GOING ON...?

AND HE CALLED HER MY BROAD... THAT'S...

I CAN'T BELIEVE THAT JERK JUST USED MY EMBARRASSING JUNIOR HIGH NICKNAME...! AAAAGH!

MOUNTAIN-BREAKER MATSUBAYASHI

YOU ALL RIGHT, MIYAZEN?

Broad (i.e. lady)

I HOPE SHE DIDN'T HEAR IT.

THAT'S WAY TOO INSULTING TO MIYAZEN!

M-

I GUESS A PRINCESS WOULDN'T KNOW THE TERM "BROAD," ANYWAY.

GOOD. LOOKS LIKE SHE DIDN'T.

THANK YOU SO MUCH...

PHEW

MATSU-BAYASHI IS SO COOL!

DAAAZE

SO COOL.

DAAAZE

AND THAT "YER BROAD" THING....!

SHE HEARD IT LOUD AND CLEAR.

SO COOL.

WHUUUMP

BLOOOOP

Miss Miyazen
Would Love to
Get Closer to You

Chapter 13 Thanks

DIIING

THIS IS ALL I COULD FIND...!

THIS IS...!

SO I CHOSE SOMETHING I THOUGHT MIGHT SUIT HIS TASTES.

Hmmm?

I LOOKED AROUND, BUT THERE WASN'T ANY MERCHANDISE FOR THE MOVIES MATSUBAYASHI LIKES...

YAKUZA HOUSE CALL 2

WHAT IF HE DOESN'T GET IT AND GOES, "HUH?" LIKE ALL THE OTHER TIMES?

BUT I'M STARTING TO FEEL RATHER NERVOUS NOW THAT I'VE GIVEN IT TO HIM...

MIYA-ZEN.

AAAAH!

AAAAH, HERE IT COMES, I JUST KNOW IT! HE MUST THINK I'M BEING WEIRD AGAIN...

THIS RULES.

Miss Miyazen
Would Love to
Get Closer to You

Chapter 14 Studying

WHY ME?
WELL,
ASIDE FROM
HUMANITIES,
MY GRADES
ARE DECENT,
I GUESS.

— This is technically a college prep school.

I CAN'T
BELIEVE I'M
TUTORING
MIYAZEN
RIGHT NOW.

THIS IS
CRAZY...

I see...

So for
this
part...

I'M GONNA DIE OF NERVES AT THIS RATE...!

SHE'S SO CLOSE.

BUT, DAMN,

I HEARD A TUTORING SESSION WOULD BRING US CLOSER,

IT'D BE LIKE THIS...

...I DIDN'T THINK

I'M SO NERVOUS, I FEEL LIKE I'M GOING TO DIE IF THIS CONTINUES...!

BUT MATSU- BAYASHI IS...

WAY CLOSER THAN I EXPECTED!

I BELIEVE IN YOU, MATSU-BAYASHI!

I'M SURE IT'LL BE FINE.

STAB

ONLY MATSU-BAYASHI DIED THAT DAY.

She trusts me...

I believe in you

I WAS GOING TO DIE IF WE DIDN'T STOP THERE...

GOODNESS, I WAS SO NERVOUS.

BADUMP

BADUMP

Miss Miyazen
Would Love to
Get Closer to You

Bonus Story
Chapter 15 Closer

I'M IN FRONT OF HIM, BUT COULD WE HAVE GOTTEN CLOSER IF I SAT NEXT TO HIM INSTEAD...?

HAVING HIM BEHIND ME IS ALREADY WONDERFUL LUCK...!

NO, NO. THAT'S ASKING FOR TOO MUCH!

YOU COMMUTE BY TRAIN, TOO, MATSU-BAYASHI?

Y-YEAH. I HAD NO IDEA...

HUH?

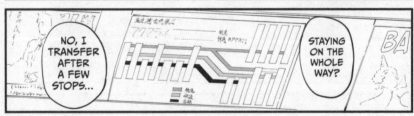

NO, I TRANSFER AFTER A FEW STOPS...

STAYING ON THE WHOLE WAY?

LINE...

FWUMP

SO YOUR HOUSE IS ON SOME OTHER...

GOT-CHA.

B-BUT THIS IS FAR TOO CLOSE!

...

I THOUGHT IT MIGHT BE RUDE NOT TO,

I SAT DOWN NEXT TO HIM!

AAH, BUT I'M A BIT SCARED TO LOOK AT HIM FROM HERE...!

O-OH DEAR, WHAT NOW? I'VE GOT TO SAY SOME-THING...

B-BREATHE. I-I'VE GOT TO CALM DOWN FIRST...

ズズ

ズズ

SHUFFLE SHUFFLE

THE DOORS WILL NOW OPEN.

ガコ

FWOOOO

MAYBE I
OUGHT
TO JUST
STAND
UP...

I WONDER
IF I'M
BOTHERING
HIM...

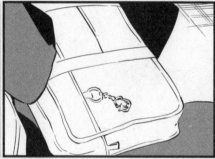

AH, THIS IS WHERE I SWITCH TRAINS.

IF YOU'LL EXCUSE ME...!

TO GET TO TALK TO HIM.

I'M LUCKY ENOUGH TO SIT IN FRONT OF HIM,

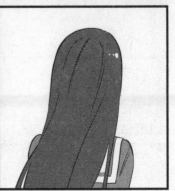

OH MY GOD, SHE WAS SO CLOSE, I THOUGHT MY HEART WAS GONNA STOP!

THE HELL WAS THAAAAAT?!

HE MISSED HIS STOP BY THREE STATIONS THAT DAY, APPARENTLY.

IF WE WERE ON THE SAME LINE, IT REALLY WOULDA....!

Miss Miyazen Would Love to Get Closer to You 1 / End